16 3. 75. ÷ 134

Euthanasia

Other Books of Related Interest:

Opposing Viewpoints Series

An Aging Population

Death and Dying

Health

Medicine

Problems of Death

Terminal Illness

Current Controversies Series

Assisted Suicide

Medical Ethics

At Issue Series

The Ethics of Euthanasia

How Should One Cope with Death?

How Should Society Address the Needs of the Elderly?

Physician-Assisted Suicide

The Right to Die

"Congress shall make no law ... abridging the freedom of speech, or of the press."

First Amendment to the U.S. Constitution

The basic foundation of our democracy is the First Amendment guarantee of freedom of expression. The Opposing Viewpoints Series is dedicated to the concept of this basic freedom and the idea that it is more important to practice it than to enshrine it.

**OPPOSING
VIEWPOINTS®
SERIES**

Euthanasia

Carrie L. Snyder, Book Editor

GREENHAVEN PRESS

An imprint of Thomson Gale, a part of The Thomson Corporation

THOMSON

GALE

Detroit • New York • San Francisco • San Diego • New Haven, Conn.
Waterville, Maine • London • Munich

Bonnie Szumski, *Publisher*
Helen Cothran, *Managing Editor*

© 2006 Thomson Gale, a part of The Thomson Corporation.

Thomson and Star Logo are trademarks and Gale and Greenhaven Press are registered trade-marks used herein under license.

For more information, contact:
Greenhaven Press
27500 Drake Rd.
Farmington Hills, MI 48331-3535
Or you can visit our Internet site at http://www.gale.com

LIBRARY OF CONGRESS CATALOGING-IN-PUBLICATION DATA

Euthanasia / Carrie L. Snyder, book editor
    p. cm. -- (Opposing viewpoints)
    Includes bibliographical references and index. 0-7377-2933-3 (lib. : alk. paper) 0-7377-2934-1 (pbk. : alk. paper)
    1. Euthanasia. 2. Euthanasia--Moral and ethical aspects. 3. Medical ethics. I. Snyder, Carrie L. II. Opposing viewpoints series (Unnumbered)
    R726.E5822 2006
    179.7--dc22
                                                        2005055110

Printed in the United States of America
10 9 8 7 6 5 4 3 2 1

Contents

Why Consider Opposing Viewpoints? 11

Introduction 14

Chapter 1: Is Euthanasia Ethical?

Chapter Preface 18

1. Christianity Condemns Voluntary Euthanasia 20
   Chris Armstrong

2. Christianity Should Condone 26
   Voluntary Euthanasia
   John Shelby Spong

3. Euthanasia Relieves Suffering 33
   South Australia Voluntary Euthanasia Society

4. Euthanasia Distorts the Meaning of Mercy 40
   Trudy Chun and Marian Wallace

5. Euthanasia Enhances Personal Freedom 53
   *Thomas Preston, Martin Gunderson, and
   David J. Mayo*

6. Euthanasia Undermines Personal Freedom 65
   John Shelby Keown

Periodical Bibliography 74

Chapter 2: Should Physician-Assisted Suicide Be Legal?

Chapter Preface 76

1. Legalizing Physician-Assisted Suicide Would 78
   Harm Society
   Margaret Somerville

2. Legalizing Physician-Assisted Suicide Would 85
   Reduce Harm to Society
   Roger S. Magnusson

3. Improved End-of-Life Care Would Make Assisted   **96**
Suicide Unnecessary
Ira Byock, interviewed by Steve Gordon

4. Improved End-of-Life Care Would Not Make   **103**
Assisted Suicide Unnecessary
Timothy E. Quill and Margaret P. Battin

5. Legalizing Assisted Suicide Would Make Killing   **114**
Too Easy
Matthew Parris

6. Legalizing Assisted Suicide Is Premature   **120**
Yvonne Mak, Glyn Elwyn, and Ilora G. Finlay

Periodical Bibliography   **126**

Chapter 3: Would Legalizing Voluntary Euthanasia Lead to Abuses?

Chapter Preface   **128**

1. Legalizing Voluntary Euthanasia Would Lead to   **130**
Nonvoluntary Euthanasia
John Keown

2. Legalizing Voluntary Euthanasia Would Not Lead   **142**
to Nonvoluntary Euthanasia
Jocelyn Downie

3. Oregon's Assisted Suicide Experience: Safeguards   **155**
Do Not Work
Oregon Right to Life

4. Legalizing Physician-Assisted Suicide in Oregon   **163**
Has Not Led to Abuses
Death with Dignity National Center

5. Legalizing Voluntary Euthanasia Would Harm   **172**
the Disabled
Barry Corbet

6. Legalizing Voluntary Euthanasia Would Not Harm   **184**
the Disabled
David J. Mayo and Martin Gunderson

Periodical Bibliography   **197**

Chapter 4: When Should Life Support Be Stopped?

Chapter Preface   **199**

1. Feeding Tubes Should Be Removed from Patients   **201**
in a Persistent Vegetative State
John Collins Harvey

2. Feeding Tubes Should Not Be Removed from   **212**
Patients Diagnosed as Being in a Persistent
Vegetative State
Wesley J. Smith

3. Doctors Should Stop Treatment That Is Futile   **224**
Kevin T. Keith

4. Doctors Should Not Deny Wanted Treatment   **229**
Lynn Vincent

5. Living Wills Allow Patients to Control When Life   **238**
Support Stops
Ruthe C. Ashley

6. Living Wills Fail to Give Patients Control over   **243**
Life Support
Angela Fagerlin and Carl E. Schneider

Periodical Bibliography   **249**

For Further Discussion   **250**

Organizations to Contact   **253**

Bibliography   **260**

Index   **265**

> *"The only way in which a human being can make some approach to knowing the whole of a subject is by hearing what can be said about it by persons of every variety of opinion and studying all modes in which it can be looked at by every character of mind. No wise man ever acquired his wisdom in any mode but this."*
>
> *John Stuart Mill*

Why Consider Opposing Viewpoints?

In our media-intensive culture it is not difficult to find differing opinions. Thousands of newspapers and magazines and dozens of radio and television talk shows resound with differing points of view. The difficulty lies in deciding which opinion to agree with and which "experts" seem the most credible. The more inundated we become with differing opinions and claims, the more essential it is to hone critical reading and thinking skills to evaluate these ideas. Opposing Viewpoints books address this problem directly by presenting stimulating debates that can be used to enhance and teach these skills. The varied opinions contained in each book examine many different aspects of a single issue. While examining these conveniently edited opposing views, readers can develop critical thinking skills such as the ability to compare and contrast authors' credibility, facts, argumentation styles, use of persuasive techniques, and other stylistic tools. In short, the Opposing Viewpoints Series is an ideal way to attain the higher-level thinking and reading skills so essential in a culture of diverse and contradictory opinions.

In addition to providing a tool for critical thinking, Opposing Viewpoints books challenge readers to question their own strongly held opinions and assumptions. Most people form their opinions on the basis of upbringing, peer pressure, and personal, cultural, or professional bias. By reading carefully balanced opposing views, readers must directly confront new ideas as well as the opinions of those with whom they disagree. This is not to simplistically argue that everyone who reads opposing views will—or should— change his or her opinion. Instead, the series enhances readers' understanding of their own views by encouraging confrontation with opposing ideas. Careful examination of others' views can lead to the readers' understanding of the logical inconsistencies in their own opinions, perspective on why they hold an opinion, and the consideration of the possibility that their opinion requires further evaluation.

Evaluating Other Opinions

To ensure that this type of examination occurs, Opposing Viewpoints books present all types of opinions. Prominent spokespeople on different sides of each issue as well as well-known professionals from many disciplines challenge the reader. An additional goal of the series is to provide a forum for other, less known, or even unpopular viewpoints. The opinion of an ordinary person who has had to make the decision to cut off life support from a terminally ill relative, for example, may be just as valuable and provide just as much insight as a medical ethicist's professional opinion. The editors have two additional purposes in including these less known views. One, the editors encourage readers to respect others' opinions—even when not enhanced by professional credibility. It is only by reading or listening to and objectively evaluating others' ideas that one can determine whether they are worthy of consideration. Two, the inclusion of such viewpoints encourages the important critical thinking skill of objectively evaluating an author's credentials and bias. This evaluation will illuminate an author's reasons for taking a particular stance on an issue and will aid in readers' evaluation of the author's ideas.

It is our hope that these books will give readers a deeper understanding of the issues debated and an appreciation of the complexity of even seemingly simple issues when good and honest people disagree. This awareness is particularly important in a democratic society such as ours in which people enter into public debate to determine the common good. Those with whom one disagrees should not be regarded as enemies but rather as people whose views deserve careful examination and may shed light on one's own.

Thomas Jefferson once said that "difference of opinion leads to inquiry, and inquiry to truth." Jefferson, a broadly educated man, argued that "if a nation expects to be ignorant and free . . . it expects what never was and never will be." As individuals and as a nation, it is imperative that we consider the opinions of others and examine them with skill and discernment. The Opposing Viewpoints Series is intended to help readers achieve this goal.

David L. Bender and Bruno Leone,
Founders

Introduction

"For advocates of both palliative care and euthanasia, the good death is one in which I make my own choices about my last days and months. In individualistic societies, the bad death is that of the person with no autonomy . . . , who cannot communicate his or her wishes or whose brain has so deteriorated that there are no wishes left."

— Tony Walter, "Historical and Cultural Variants on the Good Death," British Medical Journal, July 26, 2003.

The movement to legalize euthanasia is a fairly new phenomenon. Organizations pushing for legal euthanasia did not form until the 1930s, and it was not until the 1980s that real efforts to change the law in the United States and elsewhere began to gain attention and supporters. Two reasons account for the relatively recent debate over euthanasia: vast changes in medical technology and the patient autonomy movement.

It may seem strange that euthanasia was not more a part of life in earlier times considering that there was less that doctors could do then to fight disease and relieve pain. Bacterial and viral diseases killed young and old alike, and doctors, if available, were often powerless to bring a cure or relief. Pain and suffering were normal, expected aspects of life.

Despite these circumstances, there was no political movement afoot to legalize the means to put such suffering to an end through assisted death. The explanation for this seeming paradox is found in the circumstances at a patient's deathbed. For most people, death occurred at home, in the midst of family and community support. It was often painful but was usually not long, as treatments to preserve or prolong life were nonexistent or unavailable to most people. Religion provided a sense of meaning and the promise of better things to come in the hereafter.

In contrast, doctors now have a huge impact on curing disease or slowing its progression, and the treatments available for a chronic or terminal condition are many. Because of these medical advances, Americans no longer expect to be ill or die young, and they do not expect to have to suffer when illness strikes. However, precisely because illnesses are aggressively treated today, patients can live for months or years with debilitating and painful diseases. During the course of their illnesses, too, many people wind up in the hospital, where they often die. These facts often combine to make death a more drawn-out, clinical experience, one many Americans want to avoid. In consequence, support for euthanasia has grown.

In addition to medical advances and the changes in people's attitudes about pain and suffering, today patients expect much more control over the medical decisions made concerning them. Whereas in the past doctors made such decisions and carried out treatments without consulting the patient or the patient's family, today doctors are expected to supply patients with treatment options, and the patient ultimately decides what course of action to follow. This change reflects the recent push for patient autonomy, which in turn has developed from the rise of individualism in American society. People want to be in control of their lives, from their choice of spouse and career to where they live. It is little surprise that in a society accustomed to this type of control that the drive for euthanasia and assisted suicide has gained so much momentum. "If self-determination is a fundamental value," writes professor Dan Brock, "then the great variability among people on this question [of euthanasia] makes it especially important that individuals control the manner, circumstances, and timing of their death and dying."

Information from Oregon's experience with legal physician-assisted suicide illustrates that, indeed, control over death in the face of what may be a debilitating illness is a primary issue. Tellingly, most people who desire assisted death report their primary concern as loss of autonomy, not pain. Statistics from the Oregon Department of Human Services show that from 1998 to 2004, out of the 208 people who used the law to commit suicide, 87 percent feared losing autonomy and 80 percent feared loss of dignity. Only 22 percent cited inadequate pain control or concern that in the future their pain would not be controlled as the reason for their request.

Ironically, the debate over euthanasia emerged just when medical science promised to extend life years beyond what was possible in centuries past. The authors in *Opposing Viewpoints: Euthanasia* discuss the issues central to the debate over assisted death in the following chapters: Is Euthanasia Ethical? Should Physician-Assisted Suicide Be Legal? Would Legalizing Voluntary Euthanasia Lead to Abuses? When Should Life Support Be Stopped? As scientists continue to discover groundbreaking medical treatments, and patients continue to seek control over their lives and deaths, the euthanasia controversy will likely intensify.

OPPOSING
VIEWPOINTS®
SERIES

CHAPTER 1

Is Euthanasia Ethical?

Chapter Preface

The question of whether or not euthanasia is ethical revolves around the meaning of human existence. Those who favor euthanasia argue that human life only has meaning when the individual is free from unendurable physical and mental suffering. Euthanasia opponents contend that human life is sacred no matter what the conditions surrounding it, and that suffering can be ennobling to the human spirit. Professor Margaret Somerville explains this difference in perspective in *The Ethical Canary:*

> If we regard our bodies primarily as instruments for pleasure or for taking control, and if we value ourselves (or other people) only for what we (or they) do, not simply because we (or they) exist, euthanasia is arguably a rational response when we (or they) become weak and no longer experience pleasure or are of use. . . . If we see ourselves (and others) as having worth and dignity just because we (and they) exist, euthanasia is not acceptable because it contravenes this intrinsic worth and dignity.

As Somerville notes, suffering lies at the heart of the question, "When does life cease to have meaning?" Not only do people on both sides of the euthanasia debate argue over whether or not suffering should be endured, they also clash over whether suffering can be relieved. Most euthanasia opponents contend that physical and emotional suffering can be effectively addressed by good palliative care. Euthanasia proponents disagree, contending that many illnesses involve excruciating physical pain that cannot be relieved by modern drugs. They also argue that many patients feel the loss of dignity and autonomy associated with terminal illness more acutely than they do physical pain.

Because people disagree about the essential meaning of human life and physicians' capacity to relieve suffering, the debate over euthanasia will continue well into the future. The authors in the following chapter weigh in on this most thorny issue.

> *"Christians have usually insisted that any intentional, active termination of life rejects the truth that . . . 'God alone has sovereignty over life and death.'"*

Christianity Condemns Voluntary Euthanasia

Chris Armstrong

In the following viewpoint Chris Armstrong outlines the histori-cal opposition of Christians to euthanasia and argues that life is a gift from God and is not disposable. The author distinguishes between allowing a person to die, which is acceptable to Christians, and intentionally and actively causing death, which is unacceptable. Chris Armstrong is the managing editor of Christian History *magazine.*

As you read, consider the following questions:

1. What religion does Armstrong say has done well defining its official position?
2. What does the author say might happen to future patients if euthanasia is legalized?
3. What minority position eventually triumphed?

The case of Terri Schiavo, a severely brain-damaged Florida woman who [had] been on life support for over a decade, has reopened debate by secular and church authorities alike on questions surrounding euthanasia or "mercy killing."

The matter is admittedly not simple. But the Christian church has, at least until recent decades, spoken on it with a fairly unified voice.

Distinction Between Letting Die and Euthanasia

Here as in other issues related to human life and sexuality, the Roman Catholic Church has done a good job of defining and sticking by its official position. On the other hand, at the grassroots, more conservative Protestants than Catholics or any other group of Christians have taken an uncompromising position against euthanasia—to put it in the language of the Catholic Catechism, "an act or omission which, of itself or by intention, causes death in order to eliminate suffering."

But we must make a quick distinction: Almost all Christians have set aside as a special category cases of terminal illness in which treatment is ended in the face of inevitable death. The United Methodist Church's *Book of Discipline* states, "The use of medical technologies to prolong terminal illnesses requires responsible judgment about when life-sustaining treatments truly support the goals of life, and when they have reached their limits. There is no moral or religious obligation to use these when they impose undue burdens or only extend the process of dying."

In "Allowing Death and Taking Life: Withholding or Withdrawing Artificially Administered Nutrition and Hydration," the Evangelical Lutheran Church in America classes artificial nutrition and hydration as "medical treatment," not basic care. In cases where such treatment becomes futile and burdensome, says the document, "it may be morally responsible to withhold or withdraw them and allow death to occur."

The Islamic Position: No Euthanasia

The Shari'a (Islamic Law) listed and specified the indications for taking life (i.e. the exceptions to the general rule of sanctity of human life), and they do not include mercy killing or make allowance for it. Human life per se is a value to be respected unconditionally, irrespective of other circumstances. The concept of a life not worthy of living does not exist in Islam. Justification of taking life to escape suffering is not acceptable in Islam. . . .

There is still another dimension to the question of pain and suffering. Patience and endurance are highly regarded and highly rewarded values in Islam. . . . When means of preventing or alleviating pain fall short, this spiritual dimension can be very effectively called upon to support the patient who believes that accepting and standing unavoidable pain will be to his/her credit in the hereafter, the real and enduring life. . . .

In an Islamic setting the question of euthanasia usually does not arise, and if it does, it is dismissed as religiously unlawful.

Islamicity, "Euthanasia." www.islamicity.com.

United States law has agreed with these positions, allowing for the cessation of "heroic measures" in cases where these measures only postpone inevitable death.

But such decisions about the artificial extension of life through medical means are not really about killing, only letting die. In cases where, as the Catholic catechism puts it, hydration or feeding amount to "disproportionate means" to sustain the life of someone who already lacks cognitive function, to omit such treatment may well not amount to a direct act of killing, but rather an acknowledgement of our "inability to impede" imminent death.

Indeed, in such cases, Christians have recognized that they are in a unique position to "let go" of God's gift of life because they understand physical death as their road to another, greater life.

However, on cases marked not by the *indirect* or *passive* allowing of natural dying processes to take their course but the *direct* or *active* ending of life, the church has, at least officially, remained unified: Christians have usually insisted that any intentional, active termination of life rejects the truth affirmed in the Catholic document *Evangelium Vitae* (1995), that "God alone has sovereignty over life and death." Such acts of killing, whether "merciful" or not, unacceptably dispose of God's gift of life—over which we are not masters but only stewards.

Negative Consequences of Legalized Euthanasia

Further, both Catholic and Protestant leaders have recognized that if we legalize such active measures to end life, we not only condone individual acts that are sinful, but we also poison the care of future patients, destroying their ability to trust their own medical and emotional support network. *Any* logic condoning "mercy killing," however pure or honorable in its inception, is subject to future abuse, as medical practitioners and family members become tempted to end the lives of those whose care is taking uncomfortably high amounts of effort, time, and resources.

Even without such selfish motives, Christian critics of euthanasia point out, what happens once the door has been opened to allow criteria (say, degree of pain and suffering) by which a person may be judged justified in actively ending their own life? Those same criteria must, logically speaking, be allowed to rule similar decisions of whether to end the life of a person incapable of deciding for him or herself....

Historical Opposition to Mercy Killing

The question of whether to allow active measures by which a patient could decide whether or not to end their own life is not, as we might expect, a new one brought on by advances in technology. In the classical world, suicide was considered an honorable option. Consider the decision of the founder of stoicism, Zeno (c. 263 B.C.), to drink poison in order to avoid the suffering caused by a severe foot injury.

The Hippocratic School took a different position—one decidedly in the minority, but one that eventually, in the Christian West, won the day. The Hippocratics opposed both euthanasia and abortion. Their oath states, "I will neither give a deadly drug to anybody if asked for it, nor make a suggestion to this effect."

From the beginning, Christians have approached questions of suicide or mercy killing from the standpoint of life's sanctity as a gift from God. To end a life under any circumstance is to violate that gift, not to mention the commandment "Thou shalt not kill." It is, as the Catholic catechism says, "a murder gravely contrary to the dignity of the human person and to the respect due to the Living God, His Creator."

The Biblical basis for this "sanctity of life" position draws from the understanding of human life as gift expressed in Acts 17:25, the understanding of man created in the image of God found in Genesis 1:26–27, and the understanding of covenant in Genesis 9:5–6 and Exodus 20:13. The duty to respect human life appears in Genesis 9:5; 4:8–10, 15, and our responsibility for the life of fellow humans is taught in Genesis 4:9 and Deuteronomy 21:1–9.

This Christian position was not publicly questioned even in cases of severe suffering (though individual Christians, faced by such suffering, no doubt made decisions counter to this position) until the nineteenth century, when new anesthetic options made mercy killing more attractive in severe cases. The conversation started in the Victorian period swiftly ended at the middle of the twentieth century, however, in the face of revelations of the Nazis' programmatic eugenic killings.

It heated up again in America in the 1970s, when a young woman who went into a coma, Karen Ann Quinlan, survived for nearly a decade in what was called a "vegetative state." The New Jersey Supreme Court intervened to allow Quinlan to be removed from a respirator, and concerned observers began searching for a definition of a life no longer worth living, to justify mercy killing at least in cases where the patient could make their own decision.

In the face of Christian teachings on sanctity of life, it is hard not to see this trend towards legitimizing euthanasia or mercy killing as a strong sign that we are indeed living in a post-Christian world.

> "The choice of death with dignity, whether
> by my own hand or with the assistance
> of my physician, is a moral and a more
> godly choice than passively enduring a
> life pointlessly devoid of hope or
> meaning.'"

Christianity Should Condone Voluntary Euthanasia

John Shelby Spong

John Shelby Spong is a retired Episcopal bishop of Newark, New Jersey. In the following viewpoint he argues that the enormous medical advances of the past century necessitate a change in Christians' views of death and dying. After all, he points out, medical technology can keep patients alive long after life has meaning and hope. In Spong's view, death should not be seen as a punishment or an enemy as the Bible portrays but as a friend to be embraced. Christians have a moral obligation to share decisions about death with God; therefore, deciding to end life when it is no longer meaningful is ethical.

As you read, consider the following questions:

1. What two groups are cited by Spong as having merging values?

2. Who in the Bible does the author say was wrong about death?

3. What does Spong call "smokescreens of negativity"?

A century ago it was not an option. The final moments of life came with no heart pump or ventilators, no shrinking of tumors with radiation, no ability to cleanse a person's blood supply. Death was normally quick, since medical science had little help to offer. Then came the quantum leap in medical knowledge that expanded longevity beyond anyone's fondest dreams.

I rejoice in these incredible human accomplishments, grieving only at their limited availability across the world. Religious leaders universally applaud these medical advances that seem to validate the claim that life is sacred and calls us anew to acknowledge and even to worship the Source of this sacred life, whose name, they proclaim, is God.

New Reality for Humanity

These stunning developments, however, did not come without raising huge issues. If death is not as inescapable as it once was, a whole new level of decision making must be engaged. We are no longer simply children leaning on the Deity with no responsibility except to embrace our destiny. New dimensions of maturity become obvious. We now share in the life and death decisions that once were thought to lie solely in the domain of God.

There is no virtue in refusing to accept this new human reality. Nothing is changed by hiding our heads in the sand. This revolution has called us to frontiers where many religious ideas about the end of life must be set aside as no longer fitting our world. When that occurs, assisted suicide—under certain conditions—emerges as a new alternative for Christian people; the values marking the Christian faith and those motivating the 'Death with Dignity' movement begin to merge.

The key to this union lies in the commitment by both groups to defend the dignity and sacredness of human life. That is a rapproachment I welcome and hope to facilitate.

Death Is a Friend

As these new realities engage both groups, core definitions demand to be recast. For Christians that will not be easy. Just as we have come to believe that St. Paul was wrong in his attitude toward women and homosexuality, we now must see that he was also wrong when he viewed death as an enemy, even the "the last enemy" that had to be destroyed. When Paul wrote those words, he was under the influence of the ancient biblical myth of creation.

In that story, first thought of quite literally and later regarded as only metaphorically true, the explanation was offended that the disobedience of the first man and woman had plunged the whole world into sin, breaking the divine image in human life and causing banishment from the Garden of Eden. This fall was also said to have destroyed our immortality, causing us ultimately to die. The fact that no one escaped death was *prima facie* evidence for those like Paul, who were shaped by this defining myth, that sin was universal and death, its punishment, was the ultimate human enemy that had to be overcome.

It is easy to understand how ancient people came to these conclusions, since death was a lurking presence ready to pounce upon its victim at every stage of life. This biblical definition of death, however, is clearly wrong and must be dismissed as no longer operative. It is not even a correct metaphor.

Death is not divine punishment endured because we are fallen people. Death is a natural part of life's cycle. It must, therefore, be embraced as something good—a friend, not an enemy. Can any of us really imagine life without death being a part of it? Far from being evil, death is simply that shadow which gives life its passion, its depth, its sense of urgency. Death walks with us from the moment we are born. It pressures life. It is that reality which makes life's experiences unrepeatable. Childhood lasts but a limited time. It should be neither rushed nor restrained. The same is true for our adolescence, adulthood, and every other identifiable stage of our lives. There is only one journey through the middle years, the aging process, and into old age itself. Each stage must be grasped with vigor.

Life is meant to be lived. We are to scale its heights, plumb its depths, and taste its sweetness. Death rings the bell on all procastination. It cannot, therefore, be our enemy, something we strive to defeat. It is our friend, something we must learn to accept as an ultimate source of life's meaning. When modern medicine pushes death back in order to expand the length and quality of our existence, it is not defeating our enemy, it is revealing our holiness.

But a perilous boundary becomes visible in this new consciousness when the efforts of medical science cease expanding the length and quality of life, and begin postponing death's inevitabiliy. When that subtle and poorly defined moment comes, a new arena is entered where both a new Christian belief system and a new ethic about final things needs to be born.

Christians Must Share Decisions with God

Do we honor the God of life by extending the length of our days when the quality of our life has dissipated? Is a breathing cadaver a witness to the God of life? Should powerful narcotics be used to lessen our pain and thus to extend our days even if they rob us of the relationships which give life its meaning?

If I have a medically confirmed incurable disease, and can bear the pain of that sickness only by being placed into a kind of twilight zone, where I neither recognize the sweet smile of

A Non-Binding Gift

The Christian tradition condemning medical assistance or action which is intended to end a human life is likely to come under increasing challenge within churches and among theologians. A single example might illustrate this point. It is often argued by theologians in this context that human life is a gift, a gift from a loving God made known to us in Jesus Christ. The analogy of the gift relationship finds its foundation in God's gift of Jesus Christ as the Logos and continues in the Logos' gift of life to us.... In contrast, those who lack this faith may see human life not as a gracious gift, but as a chance by-product of a world that has meaning only if we choose to give it meaning. ...

Yet in the context of modern medicine the contrast between these two positions is not nearly so clear-cut. Christian doctors, committed to the belief that life is God-given, still face the same dilemmas about prolonging the lives of the terminally ill or permanently comatose. Gift relationships are by no means all gracious—some can be highly manipulative, especially the required gifts of submission. Gracious gifts should be treated with gratitude and responsibility, but they should not bind the one to whom they are given—it is manipulative gifts that do that. Gracious gifts can be enjoyed for a while and then shared with, or even returned with gratitude to, the giver. Gracious gifts have both giver and receiver free. Indeed when God-given life becomes nothing but a burden, it might seem appropriate to return that life prayerfully and humbly to the giver.

Robin Gill, Euthanasia and the Churches, 1998.

my wife nor respond to the touch of her hand, do I not have the ethical right to end my life with medical assistance? Can dedicated Christians step into this process and say we have now reached the point in human development where we have not just the right, but the moral obligation, to share life-and-death decisions with God? Do we not serve our deepest convictions if we decide to end our life at the moment in which its sacredness becomes compromised?

I am one Christian who wants to say not just one 'yes' to these questions, but Yes! Yes! A thousand times yes! I want to do it not in the guilt of yesterday's value system that proclaimed that only God could properly make these decisions. I went to do it, rather, as a modern Christian, asserting that human skill has brought about a new maturity in which we are both called to and equipped for the awesome task of being co-creators with God of the gift of life. As such we must also be responsible with God for guaranteeing the goodness of our deaths.

Assisted Death Is a Right That Can Be Controlled

I am not put off by the slippery slope arguments that are so often used by religious forces and the resort to fearmongering when they cannot embrace the new realities. I do not believe that this stance will lead to state-ordered executions of the elderly, or to health maintenance organizations curtailing medical payments until a quick death is achieved. I do not believe that greedy potential heirs will use this power to hasten the receipt of their inheritances. These are, in my mind, nothing but the smokescreens of negative, designed to play on the fear present when childlike dependency is threatened and when mature human decisions are mandated.

A world that is bright enough to create these opportunities is surely bright enough to control those who might misuse them. All of these abuses could be eliminated by investing this life-and-death decision solely with the affected individual. Advance directives, signed when that person is in good health should be honored. The decision-making power should reside with the individual, who alone is to be granted the legal right to determine how and when his or her life is to come to an end. That is how we will surround death with the dignity that this ancient friend deserves. I regard this choice as a right to be enshrined alongside "life, liberty, and the pursuit of happiness" at the center of our value system, a basic human freedom that we must claim.

Above all, I affirm that the choice of death with dignity, whether by my own hand or with the assistance of my physician, is a moral and a more godly choice than passively enduring a life pointlessly devoid of hope or meaning. I believe this option is rooted in the Christian conviction that life is sacred. It is thus not life denying, but life affirming. It is because we honor life that we want to end it with our faculties still intact, our minds still competent, and our dignity still respected. Assisted suicide, as a conscious choice made amid the extremity of sickness, is the way that I, as a Christian, can pay homage to the Christ who stands at the center of that faith, whose purpose, says the Fourth Gospel, was to bring life and to bring it abundantly.

To accept the responsibility of making ultimate decisions about life; to celebrate the fact that I live in an age of remarkable ingenuity; to embrace the truth that death is not our enemy but the shadow that gives life its purpose; to claim the right to determine how and when I shall die; these are the opportunities that confront people in the 21st century. I embrace them as a Christian who deeply believes in the God who is the Source of Life, who makes all life holy.

I shall live as deeply as I can while I have the opportunity. I hope to end my life as gracefully as circumstances will allow. But in both my living and my dying, even if that dying is by my own choice or hand in the face of the end of meaning and dignity, I want to assert that my decisions are within the framework of what I call Christian ethics.

> "Even with state-of-the-art palliative care many terminally ill patients will experience substantial physical and existential suffering."

Euthanasia Relieves Suffering

South Australia Voluntary Euthanasia Society

In the following viewpoint, originally published in the South Australian Voluntary Euthanasia Society (SAVES) newsletter, Julia Anaf argues that the primary reason for allowing euthanasia is to relieve suffering. When a person's pain cannot be controlled with even the best palliative care, or when a person has lost all independence and control over his or her body, permitting euthanasia is the only compassionate response. SAVES advocates for legal voluntary euthanasia for the hopelessly or terminally ill as a compassionate way to deal with futile and long-term suffering.

As you read, consider the following questions:

1. What percentage of people does the author cite as requesting euthanasia because of intolerable pain?
2. What method is used to deal with the most extreme pain, according to SAVES?
3. What nonpain syndrome does the author mention as being a major reason for euthanasia requests?

Even with state-of-the-art palliative care many terminally ill patients will experience substantial physical and existential suffering. This is also the case with the best of medical care for hopelessly ill patients who may suffer for many years with incurable and unrelievable conditions; a much longer time frame than that defined under 'terminal illness'.

Hopelessness, futility, meaninglessness, disappointment, remorse, and a disruption of personal identity are frequently experienced. The hospice ideal, therefore, to provide a pain-free, comfortable death cannot always be realised and should not be promised. It is a myth that palliative and medical care can relieve all the suffering associated with the advance of diseases like cancer, AIDS, and motor neurone disease.

Over 90% of people with terminal illness will endure their situation, but between 5–10% find it intolerable and request euthanasia. A minority of those with a hopeless illness also suffer intractable symptoms and request euthanasia.

Difficult/Impossible to Control Pain Situations

Pain, particularly that due to infiltration by cancer of extremely sensitive nerve rich areas such as the head and neck, pelvis and spine, is commonly episodic and excruciating aggravated by movement, and may be likened to a dental drill on an unanaesthetised tooth nerve.

Pain is not always adequately controlled by palliative medicine, 5–10% of cancer pain may be of this type and in some cases can only be "palliated" by producing a prolonged unconsciousness, coma or "pharmacological oblivion". This may last for days until death occurs by dehydration and circulatory collapse or retention of bronchial secretions ("the death rattle") pneumonia and pulmonary collapse.

- Raised intracranial pressure due to inoperable brain tumour

Severe head pain due to pressure on sensitive nerve structures by tumour expansion in a confined space, may be accompanied by loss of function, e.g. blindness, paralysis, incontinence

- Infiltrating head and neck cancers with/without ulceration

Some tumours fungate, hideously distort the face and produce foul odours.

- Lung Cancer infiltrating the root of the neck or chest wall and damaging sensitive nerves.

- Mesothelioma (associated with asbestosis - incurable)

Producing severe chest pain with each breath, made far worse on coughing which may be chronic and persistent - associated difficulty breathing and feelings of suffocation.

- Recurrent bowel obstruction due to widespread abdominal cancer

Diffuse deposits of cancer obstruct the bowel, causing pain, nausea and vomiting and abdominal distension - surgery may be advised which may be either futile or of only very short-term benefit. Vomiting and malnutrition lead to a kind of starvation until death.

- Pelvic cancer (bowel, bladder, prostate, uterus, ovary) may infiltrate major nerve plexuses affecting the legs or genitalia and cause severe neuropathic pain (+/− paralysis of sphincters/legs). Incontinence of urine and faeces can occur.

- Severe chronic poly arthritis with joint disintegration, which renders most movements excruciating and severely limits mobility.

- Spinal cancer with nerve root pain; vertebral collapse

Toles. © 1994 by Universal Press Syndicate. Reproduced by permission.

+/− paraplegia. One of the worst situations possible, confined to bed with - episodic excruciating neuritic pain with simple movement.

- Inoperable bladder cancer with very frequent and painful urination, often with bleeding, blockage to flow and incontinence (hence the old medical saying "Please God, do not take me through my bladder").

- Severe chronic spinal osteoporosis with vertebral collapse produces severe and unremitting pain.

- Recurrent carcinoma of the vulva with ulceration + or − invasion of bladder orurethra with loss of urine (usually acidic) across the ulcerated area.

Non-Pain Syndromes Causing Extreme Suffering

- Cachexia—commonly associated with advanced cancer, involves severe loss of appetite and weight, loss of energy in extreme degree and severe psychological "pain" (distress) due to this gross debilitation and loss of independence. Malnourished bed-bound patients are prone to develop ulcerating bedsores over bony prominences.

- Loss of appetite with intractable nausea and vomiting due to either cancer itself or drug/other therapy including chemotherapy and radiotherapy.

- Obstructing oesophageal cancer with inability to eat or even swallow saliva. Anything swallowed is vomited back.

- Chronic progressive difficulty in breathing. Possibly with severe cough, perhaps with blood. +/− severe pain with each breath or cough. Fear of suffocation causes enormous anxiety.

- Incontinence of bowel and bladder due to communication of these structures with the vagina, secondary to surgery/radiotherapy for cancer of the cervix or due to confusion and immobility.

- Chronic inexorably progressive neuropathic syndromes leading to paralysis of all limbs, loss of speech, blindness, loss of control of bowel and bladder, and perhaps inability to breathe or swallow as in multiple sclerosis, motor neurone disease. The person's body functions disintegrate, yet trapped within that shell may be a perfectly lucid mind.

- AIDS—A potentially fatal disease, often of young persons, with an horrific dying process of cachexia, immobility, incontinence and progressive loss of mental faculties.

- Total Dependence Syndrome. The loss of dignity due to loss of independence and control in the terminal decaying phase, particularly in hospital. This is a major reason for euthanasia request.

- Blockage of lymphatic or venous drainage of tissue fluid causes swelling of limbs, genitalia and face. In severe cases fluid seeps through the skin which breaks down.

- Severe stroke (such as brain stem stroke or profound dense hemiplegia) can result in permanent paralysis, inability to communicate, inability to swallow (resulting in the necessity for tube feeding), commonly followed by muscle contractures, incontinence, and bedsores, and a state of total dependence which can last for years.

- Primary or secondary cancer in the liver with vomiting and jaundice; at times painful.

- Secondary cancer in bone (commonly prostate in origin) with pathological fracture of a long bone at the site of the secondary cancer. This will not heal (eg in a hip bone or arm).

Other Intolerable Situations

- Cancer in the spine with nerve root pressure and spinal collapse

Pain will be lancinating around the body, and also possibly into the legs (as in sciatica). The pain will be provoked by simple movements such as turning in bed, coughing, urinating, using bowels. Its intensity and unpredictability make routine analgesic measures inadequate. Bedsores are a common risk. Incontinence or inability to urinate is highly likely. Every physical action, washing for example, is dreaded. Such a situation can last for months until the ravages of further cancer spread occur.

- Multiple sclerosis

Progressive loss of motor/sensory function in a haphazard way over many years leads to virtually total loss of movement. Initially wheel-chair life, later bed-bound. Total dependence, incontinence and if speech and sight are impaired, loss of even the ability to communicate. The intellect may remain unimpaired, the person is a prisoner in a body which cannot move or function in any real way.

> *"To end the life of another—or our own—because of wrenching debilitation or 'lack of quality' is to deny the reality of death."*

Euthansia Distorts the Meaning of Mercy

Trudy Chun and Marian Wallace

Trudy Chun and Marian Wallace are writers for Concerned Women for America, a conservative, pro-family, pro-life organization. In the following viewpoint they contend that euthanasia proponents mislead the public by claiming that assisted suicide is necessary to relieve patients' suffering. In fact, they argue, euthanasia does not benefit patients; rather, it helps doctors trying to reduce health care costs and patients' families, who seek relief from the distress associated with watching their loved ones die. As the public becomes more aware of the ability of modern medicine to relieve pain, support for euthanasia has been dwindling, Chun and Wallace claim.

As you read, consider the following questions:

1. What percentage of Americans aged sixty-five said they support physician-assisted suicide, according to the authors?

2. As stated by Chun and Wallace, what position has the U.S. Supreme Court taken on euthanasia?

3. What does the Hippocratic Oath state, as quoted by the authors?

Over the past several decades, America has witnessed a strange and subtle shift in how society views life. In the 1960s, the shift began as some states began to remove the criminal penalties for abortion. In the 1970s, the U.S. Supreme Court *Roe v. Wade* decision put the federal government's stamp of approval on abortion nationwide. Today, the value of life is being obscured at the other end of the spectrum as courts grant the elderly and sick the so-called "right to die."

This "right to die" movement has entered society in two forms: assisted suicide and euthanasia, with the former beginning to give way to the latter. Assisted suicide occurs when the doctor provides the patient the means to kill himself—the doctor acts as an accomplice in the self-murder, so to speak. Euthanasia is the active killing of the patient by the doctor—the physician is the murderer in this case. More often today, physicians are initiating the desire for death.

The very laws once designed to protect a person's inalienable right to life now permit the elimination of those deemed unworthy to live. And in the name of compassion, doctors trained to heal and to prolong life are shortening and even snuffing it out altogether. Killing the patient as the cure is becoming an acceptable medical procedure in some circles. Nonetheless, changing public opinion and advances in modern pain relief and end-of-life care are shifting the debate in favor of pro-life advocates.

Many Americans view physician-assisted suicide as an acceptable practice. According to a March 1999 Gallup poll, 61 percent of all Americans believe physician-assisted suicide should be legal—down from 75 percent in a May 1996 *USA Today* poll. When the issue becomes personal, fewer Americans support it. Fifty-one percent of Americans said they would not consider physician-assisted suicide to end pain from a terminal illness, while 40 percent said they would. As may be expected, support for the idea of physician-assisted suicide diminished with age in the Gallup poll. While 62 percent of those between the ages of 18 and 29 supported physician-assisted suicide, 51 percent of those aged 65 said they do.

While acceptance of euthanasia and assisted suicide has diminished somewhat, euthanasia advocates continue their campaign. The manipulation of terms in the debate reveals their strategy of courting acceptance.

Verbicide

Christian writer C.S. Lewis coined the term "verbicide" to denote the murder of a word. That is what euthanasia advocates have done with the language of "compassion" and "mercy." In order to advance their agenda with the public, euthanasia advocates are cloaking doctors' deliberate homicide of patients in rosy phrases such as quality of life, death with dignity, voluntary euthanasia, and the right to die. Even "euthanasia"—which the dictionary defines as "killing an individual for reasons considered to be merciful"—comes from two Greek words meaning "good death." But no matter what they call it, euthanasia is still murder.

Dr. Jack Kevorkian cast physician-assisted suicide and euthanasia into the national spotlight in the early 1990s. Kevorkian, a retired Michigan pathologist, claims to have helped approximately 130 people kill themselves. He calls his practice "medicide" and himself an "obitiarist." The man they call "Dr. Death" also proposes professionally staffed, well-equipped "obitoriums"—where the sick, elderly, or depressed could go to their demise voluntarily. In 1996, he opened his first suicide center north of Detroit. Fortunately, the building owner terminated Dr. Kevorkian's lease and his suicide center closed. Then, in 1999, after a nationally televised videotape showed Dr. Kevorkian ending the life of a terminally ill man, a Michigan jury convicted him and sentenced him to prison for murder.

Although Dr. Kevorkian is no longer in the national spotlight, death as the option of choice—abortion, infanticide, euthanasia and suicide—now has high-profile, big-money organizational support. Some of the most visible pro-death groups are Planned Parenthood, the National Abortion and Reproductive Rights Action League, the Hemlock Society, Choice in Dying, Americans Against Human Suffering and EXIT. Derek Humphry, cofounder of Hemlock, voices a common viewpoint: "Individual freedom requires that all persons be allowed to control their own destiny. . . . This is the ultimate civil liberty. . . . If we cannot die by our choice, then we are not free people." The decision to die is increasingly viewed as a civil "right."

Euthanasia and the Constitution

In January 1997, lawyers representing some physicians and terminally ill patients urged the U.S. Supreme Court to rule that the Constitution allows individuals the right to terminate their lives with the assistance of a physician. This action came in response to appellate court rulings in Washington and New York, where state laws banned assisted suicide. Both rulings concluded that terminally ill patients had a right to a physician-assisted suicide. In its ruling, the U.S. Court of Appeals for the Ninth Circuit in Seattle said the constitutional "liberty" reasoning in *Planned Parenthood v. Casey*, which reaffirmed a woman's "right" to choose abortion, influenced their decision. That so-called "right," the judges concluded, also applied to the end of life.

In the New York state ruling, the Federal Court of Appeals for the Second Circuit based its similar finding on the 14th Amendment's "equal protection" clause. The judges argued that terminally ill patients had the right to hasten their own

Pain Can Be Treated

The better response to patients in pain is not to kill them, but to make sure that the medicine and technology currently available to control pain is used more widely and completely. According to a 1992 manual produced by the Washington Medical Association, *Pain Management and Care of the Terminal Patient,* "adequate interventions exist to control pain 90 to 99% of patients." The problem is that uninformed medical personnel using outdated or inadequate methods often fail in practice to bring patients relief from pain that today's advanced techniques make possible. . . .

Technological advances have greatly increased the available options in administering opioids. One of these, Patient Controlled Analgesia (PCA) (a pump which can deliver a continuous infusion of a drug such as morphine, as well as allow patient-activated doses for breakthrough pain), eliminates the delay in receiving pain relief caused by having to wait for a nurse to administer the necessary medicine. . . .

We have the technology and the medicine effectively to control pain. . . . Instead of trying to legalize the killing of patients in pain, the public should be making sure that doctors are taught, and use, effective pain management.

Burke J. Balch and David Waters, "Why We
Shouldn't Legalize Assisted Suicide:
Part II: Pain Control," National Right
to Life Committee. www.nrlc.org.

death by refusing treatment. Physicians therefore could lawfully order the removal of life-support systems. In addition, doctors should not be prosecuted for actively administering lethal drugs to patients when they request help in accelerating their deaths.

The New York Times editorialized that the two courts "have is-sued humane and sound rulings." In both cases, it noted the defendants "claimed a sovereign right over their own bodies." Ernest Van Den Haag, an advocate of suicide, observed in the June 12, 1995, issue of *National Review,* "Only in our time has it come to be believed that individuals . . . own themselves. . . . Owners can dispose of what they own as they see fit."

The U.S. Supreme Court reversed both decisions, however, stating that neither state law violated the 14th Amendment of the U.S. Constitution. The Court noted, "They neither in-fringe fundamental rights nor involve suspect classifications." Furthermore, the Court argued the Equal Protection Clause of the Fourteenth Amendment "creates no substantive rights," in-cluding a so-called right to die.

Francis Schaeffer, renowned Christian philosopher and theologian, credited the influx of humanistic thought in soci-ety for the increasing disrespect for human life. "If man is not made in the image of God, nothing then stands in the way of inhumanity. There is no good reason why mankind should be perceived as special," he wrote in *Whatever Happened to the Human Race?* "Human life is cheapened. We can see this in many of the major issues being debated in our society today: abortion, infanticide, euthanasia. . . ."

Redefining Personhood

Euthanasia advocates are also redefining what it means to be a person. In their book *In Defense of Life*, Keith Fournier and William Watkins dissect "ethicist" Joseph Fletcher's 15 "indica-tors of personhood." These include: an IQ greater than 40; self-awareness; self-control; a sense of time; capability of relat-ing to and concern for others; communication; control of ex-istence and [degree of brain] function. Alarmed, Fournier and Watkins wrote: "When judged by these criteria, the preborn, newborn, and seriously developmentally disabled would be disqualified as human persons." Sufferers of dementia or anyone brain-damaged would also be non-persons. "Ethicist" Peter Singer agrees that personhood should be defined according to what we can do, rather than who we are. He has even advocated allowing parents of severely disabled infants to put their children to death in some painless way. This kind of thinking about "defective humans" is disturbingly reminiscent of the euthanasia program that accompanied the rise of Nazism.

In *A Sign for Cain*, the eminent Dr. Fredric Wertham documented exhaustively the physician-sponsored mass murder of civilians in pre–World War II Germany. Well before they were dismantled and moved to the concentration camps, gas chambers were installed in six leading psychiatric hospitals. Under the guise of "help for the dying," "mercy killings," and "destruction of life devoid of value," university professors of psychiatry, hospital directors and their staff members systematically exterminated hundreds of thousands of "superfluous people"—mental patients, the elderly, and sick and handicapped children. Criteria for such "undesirables" included "useless eaters," the unfit, unproductive and misfit.

Wertham stressed the concept of "life not worth living" was not a Nazi invention. As early as the 1920s, respected physicians wrote about "absolutely worthless human beings" and the urgently necessary "killing of those who cannot be rescued." In fact, even in 1895, a widely used German medical textbook advocated the "right to death."

However, in 1939, a note from Adolf Hitler to his own private doctor and chancellery officials extended "the authority of physicians" so that "a mercy death may be granted to patients who according to human judgment are incurably ill." Nearly the same language has been used in the various "right to die" decisions of America's high courts.

The Netherlands

In the Netherlands, the lower house of the Dutch parliament has passed a bill to permit euthanasia, paving the way for the open practice of giving doctors or relatives a "license to kill" unconscious patients. Dutch Dr. Karel Gunning, president of the World Federation of Pro-life Doctors, revealed that official figures estimate approximately 3,200 cases of euthanasia occur each year. This practice has caused a number of sick and poor Dutch to start carrying a printed card in their pockets that states they do not want doctors to put them to death. According to Dr. Gunning, the euthanasia law simply legalizes what has been done secretly for years.

"In the beginning, the explicit request of the patient was necessary," he said. "Now, one can do away with the comatose and children with severe malformations. Initially, euthanasia was allowed only for terminal patients, but later it was extended to people with psychic depression." As happened in the United States, he also believes that this "path to death" began in 1971 when the Dutch Medical Association approved abortion. This act removed "the unconditional defense of human life."

America has been sliding down the same slippery slope as Holland, spurred by the same pro-euthanasia arguments and utilizing the same tactics.

Just as Dutch doctors had secretly performed euthanasia before a law was passed allowing it, American doctors have done the same. In a Washington state survey, 26 percent of responding doctors anonymously admitted they had been asked to help a patient die. Those same doctors actually gave 24 percent of their ailing patients prescriptions that induced death. Although chronic pain was a factor, researchers found that patients were most often motivated toward suicide by nonphysical concerns, such as "losing control, being a burden, being dependent, and losing dignity."

In February 1999, columnist Nat Hentoff wrote of Oregon's legalization of physician-assisted suicide and its decision to provide the service without cost to low-income residents. Noting the cruel hypocrisy of the decision, Hentoff quoted Ric Burger, spokesman for disabled citizens in Oregon,

"The fact that the state of Oregon will not properly fund our personal-attendant services, yet will pay for us to die, amounts to nothing less than cultural genocide."

Killing People to Save Money

Secular medical ethicists also fear downright coercion in laws allowing doctors to help with suicide. They point out that not-so-subtle pressure—to save taxpayers' money—could be placed on those patients who are poorest, most isolated, and least attended. The idea is, "if you can afford it, you [can] get good care," said Zail Berry, former medical director of Hospice of Washington, D.C. "If you can't, you get a prescription for [a barbiturate] from a Medicaid doc."

Renowned medical ethicist Dr. Arthur Caplan agrees, worrying that with an aging population and an overburdened health care system, physician-assisted suicide will become not the "option of last resort ... [but] the attractive solution of first resort." In an interview with PBS's "Frontline," Dr. Caplan stated, "I worry ... that suddenly within the society, the notion will come that the older and disabled who are expensive should do the responsible thing and leave. I don't want to be in that place, and I'm not persuaded that this culture or this society isn't going to get us to that place."

In 1997, when the Supreme Court considered whether physician-assisted suicide was a constitutional right, Justice David Souter noted the slippery slope that followed. "A physician who would provide a drug for a patient to administer might well go the further step of administering the drug himself," he stated in a concurring opinion, "so the barrier between assisted suicide and euthanasia could become porous as well as the line between voluntary [and involuntary] euthanasia."

Evidence in other nations demonstrates this. The *Medical Journal of Australia* published a 1996 study of deaths in Australia. Thirty percent of all deaths are "intentionally accelerated by a doctor," by means such as withholding treatment. Moreover, only 4 percent of cases resulted from a direct response to a request from the patient—indicating the other patients were killed without consent. A patient's true desires are not usually clear.

A study in the British medical journal *The Lancet* revealed terminal cancer patients often have second thoughts about dying. Dr. Harvey Max Chochinov, a professor of psychiatry and family medicine at the University of Manitoba (Canada), said, "Will to live is a construct that is highly changeable." Surveying 168 terminal cancer patients aged 31 to 89, Dr. Chochinov and his team found "a patient could have vast temporary changes in his outlook." The study revealed causes of unwillingness to live, such as depression, were treatable.

The Hippocratic Oath

At its heart, the Hippocratic Oath taken by physicians enjoins "Do no harm" and states: "I will give no deadly medicine, even if asked." Thomas Reardon, past president of the American Medical Association (AMA) said, "Physicians are healers. . . . The inability of physicians to prevent death does not imply that they are free to help cause death."

Under-treatment has been a problem for many terminally ill patients, noted Dr. Richard Payne, chief of pain-control services at New York's Memorial Sloan-Kettering Cancer Center. The AMA has consistently opposed any attempts to legalize or promote physician-assisted suicide. In a policy paper on the issue, revised in 1999, the AMA even states, "Requests for physician-assisted suicide should be a signal to the physician that the patient's needs are unmet and further evaluation to identify the elements contributing to the patient's suffering is necessary." Physician-assisted suicide is "fundamentally incompatible with the physician's role as healer," states the AMA.

Even more encouraging are results of a 1998 survey of the 3,299 members of the American Society of Clinical Oncology

(ASCO), published in the October 3, 2000, issue of the *Annals of Internal Medicine*, concerning euthanasia and physician-assisted suicide of terminally ill cancer patients. In 1994, 23 percent of ASCO members supported euthanasia for "dying cancer patients in excruciating pain." By 1998, that number dropped to *below 7 percent.* Likewise, 22 percent of the oncologists supported physician-assisted suicide in 1998, down from 45 percent in 1994. Lead researcher Ezekiel J. Emanuel, M.D., Ph.D., stated the survey's results "emphasize the need to educate physicians about ways to provide high-quality pain management and palliative care to dying patients."

"Modern medicine was so brilliant at saving lives that we . . . forgot our traditional role of providing comfort at the end of life," said Christine K. Cassel, M.D., chair of the Henry L. Schwartz Department of Geriatrics at Mount Sinai School of Medicine. "Now we need to take the advances in modern medicine and apply them to relieving suffering." The palliative care movement is growing.

The Joint Commission on Accreditation of Healthcare Organizations (JCAHO) pushed physicians in this direction in 1999 by implementing required palliative care (pain relief) standards. It gave hospitals, nursing homes and outpatient clinics accredited by JCAHO until January 2001 to comply. The new standards require that every patient's pain be measured and relief be provided from the moment he checks into the facility. Otherwise, the health organization risks losing accreditation. Calling this a "watershed event," Dr. Russell Portenoy, pain medicine chairman of New York's Beth Israel Medical Center, commented, "No one has ever promised patients no pain." Yet euthanasia advocates have fought tooth and nail to make it easier to kill those same patients.

It is crucial the distinction be made between prolonging life artificially—with unwanted "heroic measures"—and terminating life prematurely through deliberate intervention. The first may be unacceptable to many. But the second is clearly murder. Rather, we must provide comforting care for the critically ill—food and water, pain medication, oxygen and a loving touch. Hospice programs nationwide offer medical, spiritual, legal and financial services for dying persons and their families.

In a 1994 state referendum, Oregon voters voted to allow assisted suicide. In 1997, they reaffirmed the decision by an even larger majority. At least forty-six terminally ill people have since ended their lives with the assistance of their physician. In response, Sen. Don Nickles (R-Oklahoma) inserted the Pain Relief Promotion Act into a year-end tax bill in late 2000. It passed the U.S. House but died in the Senate.

Instead of reviving the Act in the 107th Congress, profamily groups worked to have Oregon's assisted-suicide law stopped by another means.

A directive from former Attorney General Janet Reno had effectively allowed Oregon to impose physician-assisted suicide by permitting doctors to prescribe lethal doses of narcotics, claiming this is a "legitimate medical use." As soon as Sen. John Ashcroft was confirmed as President George W. Bush's attorney general, representatives from Concerned Women for America [CWA] met with Department of Justice officials to ask Mr. Ashcroft to rescind Janet Reno's order.

On November 6, 2001, Attorney General Ashcroft sent a letter to Drug Enforcement [Administration] officials to ensure that Oregon complies with federal law, which must be uniformly followed by all the states, on the proper use of controlled substances. He clarified that any person who violates the Controlled Substances Act will lose his or her license to prescribe.

"Oregon's assisted suicide rate is 42 percent higher than the nation's, and the suicide rate for those 75 or older is 63 percent higher," said Suzanne Brownlow, Director of Concerned Women for America of Oregon. "Oregon's vote for doctor-assisted suicide was a deadly mistake."

Still defiant, the pro-death movement in Oregon has, with the help of a sympathetic judge, temporarily stopped Mr. Ashcroft's order in the courts. CWA will continue to work to stop Oregon's physician-assisted suicide.

By definition, a terminally ill person's life will end—as will all our lives. The ethical challenge is how, when and at whose hand? Without question, watching a loved one waste away and suffer incurable pain is horrific. Along with them, we suffer intensely. But are we seeking to put others out of *our* misery? To end the life of another—or our own—because of wrenching debilitation or "lack of quality" is to deny the reality of death.

Fundamentally, assisted suicide and euthanasia are issues concerning morals and ethics. Indeed, the so-called "right to die" mantra has become the "duty to die." Professor David Currow, vice president of Palliative Care Australia, commented, "To make every person who's facing death think about euthanasia is an enormous impost on people who are already feeling isolated and frightened. The issue reaches to the very core of how a society views life. And it sets America sliding down a slippery slope toward destruction."

"People should be free to determine their fates by their own autonomous choices, especially in connection with private matters, such as health."

Euthanasia Enhances Personal Freedom

Thomas Preston, Martin Gunderson, and David J. Mayo.

In the following viewpoint doctors Thomas Preston, Martin Gunderson, and David J. Mayo contend that in order to respect the freedom of individuals, society must protect the right of terminally ill patients to choose euthanasia. The authors maintain that even under the stress of being seriously ill, patients can make autonomous decisions about dying, just as they do when making decisions about life-support and hospice care. Moreover, the authors point out that society encourages people to take control over other aspects of their lives, so it should also support a patient's desire to control the manner of his or her death. Preston is a professor of medicine at the University of Washington, a retired cardiologist, and a former board member of Compassion in Dying. Gunderson is a philosophy professor at Macalester College in Minnesota, and Mayo is a professor of philosophy at the University of Minnesota. He has served on the boards of the Hemlock Society and the National Death with Dignity Center.

As you read, consider the following questions:

1. What do the authors say that the principle of respect for autonomy demands?

2. What factors may limit a patient's autonomy, according to Preston, Gunderson, and Mayo?

3. On whom is the burden of proof in the debate on physician assisted dying, as asserted by the authors?

A fundamental argument in support of physician aid in dying appeals to the principle of respect for autonomy: Whenever possible, people should be free to determine their fates by their own autonomous choices, especially in connection with private matters, such as health, that primarily involve one's own welfare. Our control over our own deaths is limited by biology and a host of external influences; absent compelling considerations to the contrary, it should not be further limited by the state. This constitutes what we call the autonomy argument for physician aid in dying.

Whereas earlier critics of physician aid in dying argued that there are compelling considerations to the contrary, more recent critics have directly attacked the autonomy argument itself. Among these latter criticisms there are three distinct but overlapping threads. First, critics claim that most who would choose physician aid in dying are incapable of doing so autonomously, and hence their requests would not fall within the range of the principle of respect for autonomy. Second, it is claimed that the argument presumes excessive independence control, and self-centeredness. Third, some critics argue that the autonomy argument for physician aid in dying is self-defeating. Each of these criticisms relies on some important misinterpretation of the principle of respect for autonomy, and we find them unpersuasive.

The Principle of Respect for Autonomy

Autonomous choice is an ideal. It posits a fully informed individual who makes a reasoned and intentional choice among available options in light of that information, on the basis of his or her "true" or "authentic" values and in the absence of either internal or external coercive influences. The principle of respect for autonomy demands that others take an individual's autonomous choices seriously. It requires that autonomous choices be respected, there is compelling reason not to do so.

Although there is much debate about how to translate this ideal into practice, four points need to be noted for present purposes. First, a person influenced by others can still act autonomously, as long as the influence falls short of coercion. Second, persons who must depend on others in order to act on their choices can still act autonomously. Third, choices may be more or less autonomous, depending on whether they are more or less fully informed or more or less subject to coercive influences. Fourth, choices may be more or less important to the person making them.

These points are mirrored by important features of the principle of respect for autonomy. The principle does not require that one entirely avoid dependency or act without influence. In addition, how much weight it carries depends on the importance of the choice and on the extent to which the choice is autonomous. We routinely (if grudgingly) tolerate violations of autonomy when the choice at issue is unimportant but not when important choices are at stake.

Thus the principle of respect for autonomy demands that moral consideration be given to an individual's autonomous choices in proportion to both the degree to which those choices are autonomous and the importance (to the individual) of the values on which they are based. The principle imposes a burden that is primarily negative—a burden of noninterference. It does not by itself require us to assist others in carrying out their autonomous choices. In the case of physician aid in dying, almost no one claims that physicians have a duty to engage in the practice or that they should be required to perform aid in dying. After all, the principle protects the autonomous choices of physicians as well as patients, neither of whom should be compelled to participate in activities they find objectionable. Finally, it should be noted that respect for an individual's autonomy may be outweighed by competing considerations, such as the rights of others. Although we respect the autonomy of travelers to wander where they choose, for example, travelers may not violate the property rights of landowners by trespassing.

Given this background, the autonomy argument for physician aid in dying can be stated more fully as follows: There is a moral reason to respect others' autonomous choices, and this reason gains strength as the importance of the choice under consideration increases. An autonomous decision to hasten one's death is a profoundly important decision for a terminally ill person that involves his or her most significant values. There is therefore an extraordinarily strong moral reason not to restrict such a decision. This reason becomes even stronger when provisions are in place to ensure that the choice is indeed highly autonomous and not coerced.

The autonomy argument does not logically preclude the possibility that there may be even more compelling reasons *not* to permit an individual to act on his or her autonomous choice. However, when both principled moral disagreement and unresolved empirical issues about risks are present, as is the case in the debate over physician aid in dying, it is crucial to remember where the burden of proof falls. Current public policy and moral discussion typically assume that the burden is on those who advocate physician aid in dying. However, the autonomy argument reminds us that the burden falls on those who would *restrict* autonomy, and that this burden is very heavy indeed.

Concerns About Decision-Making Capacity

One of the most common objections to the autonomy argument for aid in dying is that terminally ill patients cannot possibly choose physician aid in dying autonomously because virtually every requirement for fully autonomous decision making—knowledge and understanding of the situation, the ability to reason, a sense of one's authentic values, and freedom from coercion—tends to be compromised in the terminally ill patient.

A variety of factors influence patients' decision-making capacity. The patient's physical condition may directly limit the possibility of autonomous choice. Physical distress resulting directly from illness can compromise autonomy, as terminally ill patients "may be experiencing too much pain, discomfort, or depression to make independent and truly voluntary decisions," [in the words Susan W.] Treatment with a mechanical ventilator or powerful drugs such as narcotics may also diminish capacity for autonomous decision making.

Patients' dependence on caregivers may also limit autonomy. The desire of many patients to have their physicians make treatment decisions for them is said to compromise patient autonomy. . . . Terminally ill patients are subject to the coercive influences of family and friends as well as those of caregivers. Those whom the patient has named as beneficiaries may subtly encourage a frightened and dependent individual to give up prematurely. A patient's vulnerability may be exacerbated by the desire not to be a burden on caregivers, a sentiment expressed by many dying patients. Some critics also contend that health care economics and the growth of managed care organizations may lead caregivers to interact with patients in ways that further compromise the patient's capacity for autonomous decision making. Treatments that might help sustain a patient's will to live may not be made available if they are costly. Patients may not receive the attention and care that would enable them to deal with their illness.

In short, opponents contend, just when they must make the most important end-of-life decisions, the capacity of many patients for autonomous decision making is impaired. Because true autonomy is unattainable in this context, critics conclude, even the principle of respect for autonomy cannot justify physician aid in dying.

These arguments apply much more broadly than their advocates realize, however. Nearly all of these challenges to capacity for autonomous decision making could apply equally to any seriously ill patient. Consider a patient facing emergency surgery, for example: Can she possibly understand the arcane technical arguments for and against a particular operation for her condition? Will the physician, or perhaps family or loved ones, subtly manipulate her in a time of crisis? All terminally ill patients who seek hospice care, or who ask not to be resuscitated or to have life-sustaining therapy withdrawn, may be influenced by the same autonomy-compromising factors that critics assert undermine that decision-making capacity of patients who request physician aid in dying—patterns of medical practices, insurance coverage, arguments by advocacy groups, and often the urgings of friends, loved ones, and attorney or pastor. Patients facing lingering deaths who might consider physician aid in dying will typically be capable of decisions at least as autonomous as those of most critically ill patients. In short, this criticism of the autonomy argument for physician aid in dying would seem to entail calling for a return to medical paternalism generally.

Those who criticize the autonomy argument for physician aid in dying on these grounds lose sight of the fact that autonomy is an ideal. They selectively set the bar for measuring actual human decisions impossibly high for physician aid in dying. They demand that choices for aid in dying be "completely" or "fully" autonomous in the sense that there be complete understanding and complete freedom from outside influences and then say that terminally ill patients do not meet

Freedom to Refuse Treatment Is No Different than Requesting Euthanasia

Although concerns about voluntariness in the context of assisted death are legitimate, they are not being raised consistently. A competent woman who is severely disabled and completely dependent upon her family might refuse antibiotics to treat a simple pneumonia in order not to burden her family. In one actual case, a 76-year-old diabetic man told his health care team that he had decided to stop dialysis. Since the man's health did not seem to warrant stopping, the health care team probed further. They discovered that he wished to stop his dialysis because he felt he was becoming an increasing burden on his wife and was overtaxing her resources. It is indeed true that some competent individuals may see themselves as a burden on their loved ones or society and refuse potentially life-sustaining treatment. However, that has not led to calls for prohibiting respect for requests to withhold treatment. Assisted suicide and voluntary euthanasia should not be treated differently.

The freedom argument applies as much to individuals consenting to the withholding or withdrawal of life-sustaining treatment as it does to assisted suicide and voluntary euthanasia. As long as it does not block accepting the former, it cannot block accepting the latter.

Jocelyn Downie, Dying Justice: Case for Decriminalizing Euthanasia, 2004.

this standard. However, the standard is one that is virtually never met in clinical medicine. . . .

The ideal autonomy that critics require for aid in dying is unreasonable because it is unattainable in any medical interaction. Yet all of us understand our circumstances more or less, and all of us are routinely subject to influences that are more or less controlling. We believe it reasonable to set the bar for patients who would opt for physician aid in dying at what is currently required for informed consent by patients who refuse life-sustaining medical treatment or ask that such treatment be withdrawn. That is, roughly, the patient must understand those facts that would be likely to influence a reasonable person. The decision must also be free from coercion and mental illness that undermines choice. None of this requires that the decision be made with perfect understanding of all possible details or that it be completely free from all potentially coercive influences, Indeed, autonomous choosers might well want to consult friends and family members and expect to be influenced by their concerns and their counsel.

Concerns About Extreme Individualism

In contrast to those who contend that persons electing physician aid in dying would be insufficiently free of external influences in their decision making, other critics hold that the autonomy argument for physician aid in dying is objectionable because it glorifies a distorted understanding of autonomy. This refers to unfettered autonomy in the sense of extreme independence, unhealthy desire for control over one's life, or self-centered individualism.

Some critics have claimed that in appealing as strongly as it does to the principle of respect for autonomy, the autonomy argument for physician aid in dying encourages extreme independence. They find this objectionable for several reasons. It may lead people to undervalue relationships and various community goods—for instance, efforts to help the less fortunate. It may also lead to a general stigmatizing of dependency on others. As a result, those who are independent might come to see the lives of those who are dependent as less valuable, while at the same time terminally ill patients who need help might opt for physician aid in dying rather than accept dependence. In this way, critics claim, the autonomy defense might ultimately function to push into seeking physician aid in dying people who otherwise might accept dependence gracefully.

These critics misunderstand the principle of respect for autonomy in two crucial ways. First, they confuse respect for autonomy with the value of independence. It is true that "autonomous" can mean "independent" and that some forms of dependency limit the capacity for autonomous choice. A person with severe disabilities, for instance, may be dependent on others in ways that limit autonomy. However, this is not relevant to the autonomy argument for physician aid in dying, which simply holds that autonomous choices should be respected. Second, the critics mistake respect for autonomy for the claim that autonomy is a value that should be maximized. The principle of respect for autonomy is not, however, a maximizing principle. In fact, there is often good reason to autonomously choose to accept dependency or limit one's autonomy in other ways—for instance, by signing an exclusive contract or joining the military. The principle of respect for autonomy holds merely that the choice to do so should be respected.

Autonomy as a Need for Control

Other critics have objected that invoking the value of self-determination to legitimate physician aid in dying glorifies an unhealthy desire for control of one's circumstances. . . . This criticism, like the preceding, misunderstands the principle of respect for autonomy. The principle holds that there is reason to respect the self-governance of individuals, but it does not specify in what this self-governance should consist. Although it might be used to exert tight control over one's life (and death), it need not be used in this way. Again, the principle of respect for autonomy does not dictate what one ought to choose; it even allows individuals to choose to surrender some degree of control over their lives or to delegate all decision making to others. . . .

Still, the positive value of being in control of one's life should not be underestimated. In fact, being an autonomous individual and acting autonomously require a high degree of self-control. This is part of what it means to be free from internal constraints. We encourage people to try to control their future health and longevity with healthy diet and exercise. We encourage control over pregnancy. Many patients choose hospice for the specific purpose of self-control. With the Patient Self-Determination Act, even the federal government encourages people to take control over end-of-life decisions by completing advance directives.

Self-Centeredness and Indifference to Others

These strands of extreme individualism and drive for control intermingle in a third critique. Critics of the autonomy argument often worry that patients might ignore the interests of others in opting for physician aid in dying. According to this third line of argument, the "extreme" exercise of autonomy represented by aid in dying engenders a moral attitude of self-centeredness that fails to take account of the interests of others. . . .

There are several general points to be made in reply to this criticism. First, the possibility that self-centered patients will make important health care decisions that adversely affect others is not unique to physician aid in dying. It is already implicit in the doctrine of informed consent. An elderly patient with pneumonia, for example, could refuse antibiotics in order to hasten her death in callous disregard for the needs of others. No one argues this is a reason for the state to police health care decisions that are selfish.

Second, this sword cuts both ways in connection with end-of-life decisions. The autonomy critics of physician aid in dying offer no reason for thinking that self-centered disregard for the interests of others would be more likely to play out one way rather than another. Terminally ill patients who are deeply loving take account of the impact their lingering deaths would have on loved ones; depending on circumstances, this might prompt them to try either to hasten or to delay their death. Conversely, selfish patients might show no regard for the interests of loved ones in deciding either to hasten death or to delay it. Furthermore, patients who desire physician aid in dying may be thwarted by the selfish whims or desires of others. This objection to physician aid in dying, then, seems diametrically opposed to the concern that terminally ill patients might be pressured into opting for it because loved ones have made their wishes known.

This brings us to a third reply: Although as a general rule people should be respectful of the feelings of those close to them, in the final analysis the choice is that of the individual. Individual freedom to marry, worship, or live where one chooses—and indeed, even refuse life-prolonging therapies as one sees fit—all are personal freedoms that may be exercised in ways that show selfish disregard for the feelings and concerns of others. Yet it would never occur to us to characterize our institutionalized respect for these freedoms as the abandonment of "compassionate caring to the end" or as a battle cry that drowns out the protestations of friends and relatives who may be affected. Rather, these are basic freedoms that we encourage people to exercise responsibly—with the full realization that sometimes they will fail to do so. . . .

The Burden of Proof

The principle of respect for autonomy has played an important role in medical practice. It justifies the requirement of informed consent in both therapeutic and research contexts. It also forms the basis of the autonomy argument for physician aid in dying. While critics of this argument have offered a range of objections, they make several characteristic mistakes. Some confuse the ideal of autonomous choice with the operational standard of autonomous choice that is incorporated in workable health care policies. Some confuse the principle of respect for autonomy with a particular substantive view of the good that places a premium on rugged individualism. Some critics mistakenly assume that the principle requires maximizing autonomy; rather, it provides reason to respect autonomous choice even when someone chooses to limit his or her own autonomy. Some critics mistakenly interpret the principle as stating an absolute right; on this interpretation, the principle is clearly unacceptable. On our interpretation, however, the principle imposes a burden of proof on those who would restrict autonomous choice. It does this in a way that takes account of context, and the burden it imposes may be more or less heavy. Advocates of physician aid in dying believe that in the particular context of terminally ill patients autonomously choosing on the basis of deeply held values, the heavy burden on those who would prohibit physician aid in dying cannot be met.

> *"The value of autonomy lies not in making just any choice but [in making] choices which are consistent with a framework of sound moral values."*

Euthanasia Undermines Personal Freedom

John Shelby Keown

Author John Shelby Keown argues in the following viewpoint that autonomy, or personal freedom, is not an absolute right to be respected above all else. With the right to choose, he says, comes responsibility to make choices that do not harm the individual choosing or others. While autonomy is important, it is not the only value. Therefore, society does not have to legalize voluntary euthanasia on this basis. Keown also points out that requests for euthanasia may not be made freely since a patient is often in distress when a request is made. Keown is a senior lecturer in the faculty of law at the University of Cambridge in the United Kingdom. He has also authored Abortion, Doctors and the Law *(1988) and* Euthanasia Examined *(1995).*

As you read, consider the following questions:

1. According to the author, what choices, or "exercises of autonomy," merit respect?

John Shelby Keown, *Euthanasia, Ethics, and Public Policy: An Argument Against Legalisation.* New York: Cambridge University Press, 2002. Copyright © 2002 by Cambridge University Press. Reproduced by permission.

2. What other value is in competition with the right of self-determination?

3. What are some impairments to true autonomy for those with a terminal illness?

The belief that in some circumstances death is better than life, that life is no longer worth living, is an important strand in the argument for VAE [Voluntary Active Euthanasia]. Another strand, hardly less central, is that VAE respects a patient's right to autonomy or self-determination. The bulk of those campaigning for relaxation of the law weave the two strands together. They stress that they support only *voluntary* euthanasia: euthanasia is only ever justifiable *at the request of the patient* as no one but the patient is in a position to judge the worthwhileness of his own life. Only if the *patient* decides that life has lost its value and asks for VAE should it be performed.

Traditional Views Now Rejected

Given the rise, particularly in the West, of an almost absolute respect for personal autonomy and the decline of established religious belief on which respect for the inviolability of life has traditionally been based, it is hardly surprising that support for VAE appears to have grown substantially. The traditional consensus has been undermined by liberal pluralism. Many people now reject traditional views about the inviolability of life—views which they often criticise as 'religious', 'authoritarian', 'absolutist' and unfairly 'imposed' by the law on non-believers. They support the relaxation of the law so as to allow individuals to make their own personal decisions about what to value and how to act, particularly when the decision affects so fundamental and personal a matter as when and how to die. If, they argue, a patient thinks that VAE is immoral, he need not ask for it. If, on the other hand, a patient thinks that continued life in a suffering or incapacitated state is an indignity, inconsistent with his own assessment of what makes life worth living, he should be allowed to obtain VAE. As [Ronald Dworkin, a] leading liberal advocate of relaxation has (rather emotively) put it: 'Making someone die in a way that others approve, but he believes a horrifying contradiction of his life, is a devastating, odious form of tyranny.'

The Purpose and Value of Autonomy

While placing a high value on autonomy, opponents of VAE argue that its importance is exaggerated by supporters of VAE. The value of individual choice lies, opponents would argue, in the fact that it is through our choices that we are able to promote our own flourishing as human beings (and that of those around us). Such choices, moreover, serve to reinforce dispositions to act in ways conducive to our flourishing. For our choices have internal as well as external effects and serve to shape our character. A's murder of B results not only in B being murdered but in making A a murderer. As the ancient adage attests, an act tends to form a habit, a habit tends to form a character, and a character tends to form a destiny.

The capacity to choose brings with it the responsibility of making not just any old choice, but choices that do in fact promote, rather than undermine, human flourishing. Given the legitimate diversity of lifestyles and life-choices which are consistent with human flourishing, many choices are consistent with human well-being. We should, therefore, think carefully before restricting another's autonomy. But it is difficult to see why patently immoral choices, choices clearly inconsistent with human well-being, merit any respect.

In other words, an exercise of autonomy merits respect only when it is exercised in accordance with a framework of sound moral values. For example, A's decision to murder B is an exercise of autonomy, but it hardly merits respect since it breaches a grave moral norm. This is particularly clear when the decision, such as a decision to murder, seriously harms another person. But it is also true when the decision is morally wrong, whether or not it 'harms' another and whether or not the 'victim' consents. Should we respect decisions to buy and smoke 'crack' cocaine? Or to perform the mutilating procedure of 'female circumcision' on a consenting woman? Or to kill oneself? Opponents of absolute respect for individual autonomy could also cite instances of individual autonomy being restricted by the criminal law even when the act in question is not seriously immoral, such as driving a car without a seatbelt. They would argue that autonomy, far from being a self-justifying end in itself, is more like the pointer in a compass. The pointer itself is of little value, indeed makes little sense, in the absence of the points of the compass. When the pointer indicates a morally valuable course—and there may be a number of morally valuable courses—the choice merits respect. But when the choice is immoral, whether because it would harm another, or oneself, what claim to moral respect can it have? This is *not* to say that *all* immoral choices should be overridden by the law—the law is, for one thing, too blunt an instrument for that—merely that such choices cannot command moral react. Those making immoral choices certainly have no right to be assisted in carrying them out.

The Right to Choose What?

Opponents of VAE would add that much contemporary talk about autonomy consists of little more than the naked assertion that a person's choice merits respect *simply because it is his choice, whatever that choice may be.* They would add that supporters of VAE who reject the inviolability of life as being 'absolutist' are hypocritically trying to supplant it with another moral absolute: an unqualified respect for individual choice, focusing on a self-justifying 'right to choose' rather than on what it is right to choose. The 'right to choose x' often serves as a slogan with powerful emotional appeal. But crude slogans are no substitute for rational reflection, and one can hardly sensibly assert a right to choose 'x' until one has considered whether it is right to choose 'x'; to do otherwise is simply to beg the question. Is there a 'right to choose . . . paedophilia'? Or a 'right to choose . . . cruelty to animals'? Does the mere fact that someone *wants* to blind ponies or to have sex with children carry any moral weight? The 'right to choose' only arguably makes any moral sense in the context of a moral framework which enables us to discern what it is *right* to choose and what choices will in fact promote human flourishing. And not only *our* flourishing, but that of others. For we do not live as atomised individuals, as much loose talk about absolute respect for personal autonomy seems to assume, but in community, where our choices can have profound effects not only on ourselves but on others. As Professor [Alexander] McCall Smith has pertinently observed, we live our lives in the moral company of others, with whom our lives constantly intersect. He cautions that regarding autonomy as the supreme value invites moral pluralism, which easily becomes moral relativism, which is corrosive of moral community. If, by contrast, autonomy is regarded as but one of several important values, then the case for VAE becomes subject to a consideration of those other values.

One of those values is, of course, the value of human life. If the principle of the inviolability of life is accepted, and it has hitherto been a hallmark of civilised societies, its implications for the right to self-determination are patent. If it is seriously immoral intentionally to kill an innocent person, it is difficult to see how a choice to kill, whether another or oneself, can command moral respect. As the Anglican and Catholic bishops stated in their joint submission to the House of Lords Select Committee on Medical Ethics, autonomy is not absolute and is valid 'only when it recognises other moral values, especially the respect due to human life as such, whether someone else's or one's own.' Indeed, the argument continues, given the fundamental value of life, society is fully justified in

Not Free Choice

We believe that as long as disabled people are viewed as a suffering entity, as an object of charity, as a life not worth living, we cannot accept the broadening of our access to death. It is not without a reason that studies show that the support for euthanasia is greatest among the healthy and young and lowest among the elderly and frail and the ones with the least control over their lives.

We believe that the legalization of euthanasia will force people to be euthanized in a misbegotten effort to do the right thing: save their loved ones from financial ruin, remove family members from the care taker role, cease to be a burden on the state....

We believe that the majority of death wishes are based on a lack of support and understanding for the individual by society.

We believe that euthanasia is another technique to free society of unwanted members of society among them disabled people and another expression of the ableism in western societies.

Dr. Gregor Wolbring, "Why Disability Rights Movements
Do Not Support Euthanasia: Safeguards Broken Beyond
Repair," Independent Living Institute.
http://www.independentliving.org/docs5/wolbringeuthanasia.html.

using the criminal law to deter the implementation of such choices. This is not to say that society must use the law against attempted suicides, who typically need understanding and help rather than condemnation and punishment, but simply that it remains reasonable to use it against those who would assist or encourage suicide.

Opponents of VAE would conclude that, just as the patient's life is not the highest moral value requiring preservation at all costs, neither is the patient's self-determination a moral absolute requiring respect in all circumstances, and certainly not when it involves a choice to kill, whether oneself or another.

The Right to Refuse Futile or Excessively Burdensome Treatments

What role, then, would opponents of VAE accord to individual autonomy at the end of life? While denying that it could ever be right for a patient to judge that his life was no longer worth living, they would defend the patient's right to judge whether a proposed treatment would be beneficial, as for example by improving the quality of his life.

In determining whether a proposed treatment would involve excessive burdens to a particular patient, the views of the patient are clearly crucial. People differ, for example, in their ability to tolerate pain, and what may be excessively painful for one patient may not be so for another. Indeed, the distinctions between proportionate and disproportionate treatments were devised by moral thinkers not primarily for the purposes of healthcare professionals faced with decisions about which treatments they ought to offer, but for patients facing decisions about which treatments they ought to accept. Moreover, the responsibility for safeguarding and promoting the good of health lies primarily with the *patient*, not with the doctor, at least where the patient is able to make his own decisions. Choices by patients which promote the good of health therefore merit respect and it is reasonable to allow patients considerable leeway, given the considerable variation between patients, in deciding what treatments they would find too onerous.

Requests for Euthanasia May Not Be Autonomous

There is a further objection that opponents of VAE could raise. *Just how autonomous* are requests for VAE likely to be? Requests are likely to emanate from patients experiencing significant distress at the close of their lives, whose judgment is impaired by the painful effects of terminal illness, clouded by the side-effects of medical treatment, and warped by clinical depression or 'demoralisation', [in the words of David Kissane and colleagues]. Even if a patient's capacity for choice were unaffected, how informed is he likely to be about the diagnosis and prognosis and about alternatives such as palliative care? Is there not a genuine danger that many patients would request VAE not because of a clear-headed evaluation that it was the best option for them but because they felt abandoned, or an unwanted burden on relatives, medical and nursing staff, or society? In short, how many requests would reflect the *truly* autonomous wishes of the patient? Significantly, an impressive body of research indicates that a majority of patients who request VAE are indeed suffering from clinical depression or inadequately treated symptoms. Commenting on the psychiatric literature, two experts [Annette Street and David Kissane] have observed: 'Studies exploring the motivations that lead to a desire for euthanasia have highlighted the prominent role of depression in its development' ['Dispensing Death, Desiring Death: An Exploration of Medical Roles and Patient Motivation during the Period of Legalised Euthanasia in Australia'].

The second major argument for VAE, that it respects individual autonomy, is too often advanced as if it were an obvious conclusion rather than a controversial proposition. The counter-argument is that many requests for VAE are not truly autonomous but result from depression or inadequate palliative care and that, in any event, the value of autonomy lies not in making just *any* choice but choices which are consistent with a framework of sound moral values. If this is so, then talk of 'respect for personal autonomy' tends to distract attention from the *fundamental* moral question, raised by the first argument, . . . which is whether doctors are justified in intentionally terminating the lives of patients, even on request.

Periodical Bibliography

The following articles have been selected to supplement the diverse views presented in this chapter.

David P. Gushee   "Killing with Kindness," *Christianity Today,* December 2004.

Herbert Hendin   "The Practice of Euthanasia," *Hastings Center Report,* July 1, 2003.

Nat Hentoff   "Challenging Singer," *Free Inquiry,* Winter 2001.

Garret Keizer   "Life Everlasting: The Religious Right and the Right to Die," *Harper's Magazine,* February 2005.

Bob Lane   "Active and Passive Euthanasia: Is There a Moral Distinction?" *Humanist in Canada,* Spring 2005.

Ian Lawton   "The Sanctity of Death: Theism, War, and Euthanasia," *St. Matthew-in-the-City Anglican Church E-zine,* Auckland, New Zealand, March 16, 2003. http.//st.matthews.org.

Aaron Parry   "A Jewish Perspective on Euthanasia," *Complete Idiot's Guide to the Talmud.* www.ravparry.com.

Rachael Patterson and Katrina George   "Euthanasia and Assisted Suicide: A Liberal Approach Versus the Traditional Moral View," *Journal of Law and Medicine* , May 2005.

Michael Petrou   "A Time to Die" *Maclean's,* September 5, 2005.

Mark Pickup   "Unspeakable Conversations for Good Atheists," *Human Life Review,* Spring 2003.

Peter Singer   "Voluntary Euthanasia: A Utilitarian Perspective," *Bioethics,* October 2003.

Barbara Smoker   "On Advocating Infant Euthanasia," *Free Inquiry,* December 2003.

Tony Walter   "Historical and Cultural Variants on the Good Death," *British Medical Journal,* July 26, 2003.

OPPOSING
VIEWPOINTS®
SERIES

CHAPTER 2

Should Physician-Assisted Suicide Be Legal?

Chapter Preface

Supporters of physician-assisted suicide (PAS) have attempted to legalize it in many states, but with the exception of Oregon, they have been unsuccessful. Public opinion polls show that a majority of Americans favor legalized PAS in general, but when asked to vote for or against it, they oppose it. In four states—Washington, California, Michigan, and Maine—proposals to legalize PAS were defeated by margins as wide as 71 percent against and 29 percent for (in Michigan in 1998), and as narrow as 51 percent against and 49 percent for (in Maine in 2000). Proponents' inability to pass another Oregon-style law has perplexed those in favor of legalization and has led to speculation about why this occurs.

It seems that in abstract terms, the "right to die" and "right to choose the timing of one's death" sound appealing to many people. However, when an initiative is actually written, the difficulty is in the details. Americans asked to vote on the initiative ask, Who actually qualifies for PAS? What is the role of doctors in the process? How much is the government involved in these decisions? What kinds of safeguards would be put in place? Voters seem much more hesitant to make assisted suicide legal when they think about the actual logistics of legalization. Yale Kamisar, a prominent opponent of euthanasia, notes in *The Case Against Assisted Suicide*, "It is much easier to sell the basic notion of assisted suicide than to sell a complex statute making the idea law. . . . People start worrying about whether the measure provides too few procedural safeguards or too many."

Americans' ambivalence about euthanasia centers on their compassion for those suffering from a terminal illness. Generally, Americans want that suffering to be relieved, and if palliative care is inadequate to do so, they favor the idea of PAS. However, the same compassion leads to doubts about how legalized PAS would be regulated so that the terminally ill and other vulnerable people are not killed against their wishes. People fear that voluntary euthanasia would inevitably lead to involuntary euthanasia.

The following chapter explores whether assisted suicide should be legal. Because of the complicated nature of compassion and the difficulty of crafting sound laws, Americans' ambivalence about physician-assisted suicide is likely to continue.

"To legalize euthanasia would damage
important, foundational societal values
and symbols that uphold respect for
human life."

Legalizing Physician-Assisted Suicide Would Harm Society

Margaret Somerville

In the following viewpoint Margaret Somerville argues that legalizing euthanasia would be harmful to society because it would undermine citizens' shared respect for human life. She also claims that legalizing euthanasia would harm the medical profession by allowing doctors to kill society's most vulnerable members, thereby breeding mistrust of the medical establishment. Margaret Somerville is Gale Professor of Law at the McGill University Centre for Medicine, Ethics, and Law in Montreal, Canada. She is also the author of The Ethical Canary: Science, Society, and the Human Spirit *and* Death Talk: The Case against Euthanasia and Physician-Assisted Suicide.

As you read, consider the following questions:

1. On what basis does Somerville say that euthanasia cannot be just a private matter of self-determination?
2. What are the two views of human life explained by the author?

Margaret Somerville, "The Case Against: Euthanasia and Physician-Assisted Suicide," *Free Inquiry*, 2003, vol. 23, Spring 2003. Copyright © 2003 by the Council for Democratic and Secular Humanism, Inc. Reproduced by permission of the author.

3. What, in the author's view, would be difficult to communicate to future physicians if euthanasia were legal?

There are two major reasons to oppose euthanasia. One is based on principle: it is wrong for one human to intentionally kill another (except in justified self-defense, or in the defense of others). The other reason is utilitarian: the harms and risks of legalizing euthanasia, to individuals in general and to society, far outweigh any benefits.

When personal and societal values were largely consistent with each other, and widely shared because they were based on a shared religion, the case against euthanasia was simple: God or the gods (and, therefore, the religion) commanded "Thou shalt not kill." In a secular society especially one that gives priority to intense individualism, the case for euthanasia is simple: Individuals have the right to choose the manner, time, and place of their death. In contrast, in such societies the case against euthanasia is complex.

Definitions are a source of confusion in the euthanasia debate—some of it deliberately engendered by euthanasia advocates to promote their case. Euthanasia is "a deliberate act that causes death undertaken by one person with the primary intention of ending the life of another person, in order to relieve that person's suffering" [as written by M. Somerville in *Death Talk*]. Euthanasia is not the justified withdrawing or withholding of treatment that results in death. And it is not the promotion of pain relief, even if it could or would shorten life, provided the treatment is necessary to relieve the patient's pain or other serious symptoms of physical distress and is given with a primary intention of relieving pain and not of killing the patient.

Euthanasia's Impact on Society

To legalize euthanasia would damage important foundational societal values and symbols that uphold respect for human life. With euthanasia, how we die cannot be just a private matter of self-determination and personal beliefs, because euthanasia "is an act that requires two people to make it possible and a complicit society to make it acceptable," [according to D. Callahan in "When Self-Determination Runs Amok"]. The prohibition on intentional killing is the cornerstone of law and human relationships, emphasizing our basic equality.

Medicine and the law are the principle institutions that maintain respect for human life in a secular, pluralistic society. Legalizing euthanasia would involve—and harm—both of them. In particular, changing the norm that we must not kill each other would seriously damage both institutions' capacity to carry the value of respect for human life.

To legalize euthanasia would be to change the way we understand ourselves, human life, and its meaning. To explain this last point requires painting a much larger picture. We create our values and find meaning in life by buying into a "shared story"—a societal-cultural paradigm. Humans have always focused that story on the two great events of each life, birth and death. Even in a secular society—indeed, more than a religious one—that story must encompass, create space for, and protect the "human spirit." By the human spirit, I do not mean anything religious (although this concept can accommodate the religious beliefs of those who have them). Rather, I mean the intangible, invisible, immeasurable reality that we need to find meaning in life and to make life worth living—that deeply intuitive sense of relatedness or connectedness to others, the world, and the universe in which we live.

Two Views of Human Life

There are two views of human life and, as a consequence, death. One is that we are simply "gene machines." In the words of an Australian politician, when we are past our "best before" or "use by" date, we should be checked out as quickly, cheaply and efficiently as possible. That view favors euthanasia. The other view sees a mystery in human death, because it sees a mystery in human life, a view that does not require any belief in the supernatural.

Euthanasia is a "gene machine" response. It converts the mystery of death to the problem of death, to which we then seek a technological solution. A lethal rejection is a very efficient, fast solution to the problem of death—but it is antithetical to the mystery of death. People in postmodern societies are uncomfortable with mysteries, especially mysteries that generate intense, free-floating anxiety and fear, as death does. We seek control over the event that elicits that fear; we look for a terror-management or terror-reduction mechanism. Euthanasia is such a mechanism: While it does not allow us to avoid the cause of our fear—death—it does allow us to control its manner, time, and place—we can feel that we have death under control.

Research has shown that the marker for people wanting euthanasia is a state that psychiatrists call "hopelessness," which they differentiate from depression—people have nothing to look forward to. Hope is our sense of connection to the future; hope is the oxygen of the human spirit. Hope can be elicited by a sense of connection to a very immediate future, for instance, looking forward to a visit from a loved person, seeing the sun come up, or hearing the dawn chorus. When we are dying, our horizon comes closer and closer, but it still exists until we finally cross over. People need hope if they are to experience dying as the final great act of life, as it should be. Euthanasia converts that act to an act of death.

A more pragmatic, but nevertheless very important, objection to legalizing euthanasia is that its abuse cannot be prevented, as recent reports on euthanasia in the Netherlands have documented. Indeed, as a result of this evidence some former advocates now believe that euthanasia cannot be safely legalized and have recently spoken against doing so.

To assess the impact that legalizing euthanasia might have, in practice, on society, we must look at it in the context in which it would operate: the combination of an aging population, scarce health-care resources, and euthanasia would be a lethal one.

Euthanasia's Impact on Medicine

Advocates often argue that euthanasia should be legalized because physicians are secretly carrying it out anyway. Studies purporting to establish that fact have recently been severely criticized on the grounds that the respondents replied to questions that did not distinguish between actions primarily intended to shorten life—euthanasia—and other acts or omissions in which no such intention was present—pain-relief treatment or refusals of treatment—that are not euthanasia. But even if the studies were accurate, the fact that physicians are secretly carrying out euthanasia does not mean that it is right. Further, if physicians were presently ignoring the law against murder, why would they obey guidelines for voluntary euthanasia?

Euthanasia "places the very soul of medicine on trial," [according to W. Gaylin and colleagues in "Doctors Must Not Kill"]. Physicians' absolute repugnance to killing people is necessary if society's trust in them is to be maintained. This is true, in part, because physicians have opportunities to kill not open to other people, as the horrific story of Dr. Harold Shipman, the British physician-serial killer, shows.

How would legalizing euthanasia affect medical education? What impact would physician role models carrying out euthanasia have on medical students and young physicians? Would we devote time to teaching students how to administer death through lethal injection? Would they be brutalized or ethically desensitized? (Do we adequately teach pain-relief treatment at present?) It would be very difficult to communicate to future

Damaging the Doctor-Patient Relationship

Legalization of euthanasia will lead to a broader acceptance and increased practice of euthanasia, which will change the nature of the patient-physician relationship as well as the character of terminal palliative care. The acceptance of euthanasia as a treatment option is incompatible with the fundamental role of the physician as healer who is unconditionally devoted to respect for the life of his patients. Since the physician's role and the extent of his or her competence is regulated by law, such a fundamental change in the physician's competence concerns society as a whole and cannot be considered as a private matter for patients and physicians.

Henk Jochemson, Ethics & Medicine,
Spring 2001.

physicians a repugnance to killing in a context of legalized euthanasia.

Physicians need a clear line that powerfully manifests to them, their patients, and society that they do not inflict death; both their patients and the public need to know with absolute certainty—and to be able to trust—that this is the case. Anything that would blur the line, damage that trust, or make physicians less sensitive to their primary obligations to protect life is unacceptable. Legalizing euthanasia would do all of these things.

Euthanasia Hurts Society's Vulnerable Members

Euthanasia is a simplistic, wrong, and dangerous response to the complex reality of human death. Physician-assisted suicide and euthanasia involve taking people who are at their weakest and most vulnerable, who fear loss of control or isolation and abandonments—who are in a state of intense "pre-mortem loneliness" [coined by J. Katz in *The Silent World of Doctor and Patient*]—and placing them in a situation where they believe their only alternative is to be killed or kill themselves.

Nancy Crick, a sixty-nine-year-old Australian grandmother, recently [May 2002] committed suicide in the presence of over twenty people, eight of whom were members of the Australian Voluntary Euthanasia Society. She explained: "I don't want to die alone." Another option for Mrs. Crick (if she had been terminally ill—an autopsy showed Mrs. Crick's colon cancer had not recurred) should have been to die naturally with people who cared for her present and good palliative care.

Of people who requested assisted suicide under Oregon's Death with Dignity Act, which allows physicians to prescribe lethal medication, 46 percent changed their minds after significant palliative-care interventions (relief of pain and other symptoms), but only 15 percent of those who did not receive such interventions did so.

How a society treats its weakest, most in need, most vulnerable members best tests its moral and ethical tone. To set a present and future moral tone that protects individuals in general and society, upholds the fundamental value of respect for life, and promotes rather than destroys our capacities and opportunities to search for meaning in life, we must reject euthanasia.

"A statutory regime provides the opportunity for law to re-regulate euthanasia and to protect patients through . . . safeguards."

Legalizing Physician-Assisted Suicide Would Reduce Harm to Society

Roger S. Magnusson

Roger S. Magnusson, an associate professor at the University of Sydney Law School in Australia, makes a case in the following viewpoint for legalizing physician-assisted suicide (PAS) in the United States. He claims that PAS should be legalized so that the problems associated with underground euthanasia, including botched attempts to aid death, will end. He argues that legalization of PAS will do less damage to society than do the covert actions of doctors participating in PAS illegally. According to Magnusson, if PAS is legalized, safeguards can be put in place to regulate the practice and protect patients. This viewpoint is excerpted from a longer article based on Magnusson's detailed interviews with forty-nine doctors, nurses, and therapists involved in underground euthanasia or assisted suicide. His findings are also the foundation of his book Angels of Death: Exploring the Euthanasia Underground.

As you read, consider the following questions:

Roger S. Magnusson, "'Underground Euthanasia' and the Harm Minimization Debate," *Journal of Law, Medicine, and Ethics*, vol. 32, Fall 2004, pp. 486–93. Copyright © 2004 by the *Journal of Law, Medicine, and Ethics*. Reproduced by permission.

1. What percentage of oncologists has been involved in euthanasia and assisted suicide, as cited by Magnusson?
2. What does the author say is the most striking problem associated with covert physician-assisted suicide?
3. How does Magnusson address opponents' slippery slope argument?

Joseph (a pseudonym) is an eminent HIV/AIDS physician, one of many doctors and nurses in America today who have assisted a patient to die. In terms of frequency, Joseph's career is middling. He claimed to have written "five to ten" lethal prescriptions during our interview, but that was years ago and he has doubtless been involved since then. Others I interviewed had been involved dozens of times. "I'm not here to cure everybody," Joseph says. "Death is a natural part of the cycle of life, and as a physician I have an opportunity to grant people peace and comfort in their death, and it's something that I'm not unwilling or afraid to do."

The "euthanasia underground" is the underbelly of medicine and nursing. At the empirical level, its presence is not seriously open to challenge. Surveys consistently demonstrate that a significant percentage of doctors comply with patient requests by taking active steps to intentionally hasten the patient's death, whether by prescribing lethal quantities of drugs for self-administration by the patient (physician-assisted suicide, or PAS), or by the direct administration of lethal injections or infusions at the patient's request (active voluntary euthanasia, or AVE).

A national survey of 1902 American physicians found that 3.3 percent had written at least one "lethal prescription," while 4.7 percent had provided at least one lethal injection. A survey of American oncologists found that 3.7 percent had performed euthanasia, while 10.8 percent had assisted suicide. In a random sample of American physicians, 44.5 percent favored the legalization of physician-assisted suicide (PAS) (33.9 percent were opposed). . . .

Despite the growing body of survey evidence, remarkably little is known about the circumstances in which doctors participate in PAS/AVE, whether their assistance results in what is perceived to be a good death for the patient, and the long-term impact of involvement on health care providers themselves. . . .

The "Euthanasia Underground"

While it does not provide a basis for broad empirical claims, the testimony of interviewees provides a window into the variety of ways that health professionals assist patients to die, the semi-organized nature of covert PAS/AVE and the factors motivating involvement. For many I spoke to, the interview provided a safe place from which to challenge the complacency and silence of the medical and nursing professions. Some saw themselves at the vanguard of a new ethic of caring: one that encompassed assisted death as part of their professional role. Others were clearly stressed, fatigued, and did not even try to make sense of it anymore.

Despite their mostly good intentions, the picture that emerged from the interviews is a disturbing one. Take Stanley, a therapist and former priest, who presided over the death of a patient who swallowed fifteen Seconal tablets (a barbiturate), but who failed to take an anti-nausea drug to prevent vomiting. The patient died, but only after reingesting his own vomit.

In many cases, doctors and nurses miscalculated the dosages required to achieve death and resorted in panic to suffocation, strangulation, and injections of air in their desperate efforts to finish the job. Of the eighty-eight detailed narratives that interviewees gave as illustrations of their PAS/AVE credentials, nearly twenty percent involved "botched attempts.". . .

The most striking feature of covert PAS/AVE is the complete absence of guidelines or stable criteria for deciding when it is appropriate to proceed. One doctor injected a young man on the first occasion they met, despite concerns from close friends that the patient was depressed. . . . [One] experienced HIV/AIDS physician wrote a lethal prescription for his hairdresser's partner, whom he had never met, admitting that "there was no assessment involved whatsoever.". . .

Covert PAS/AVE has spawned a culture of deception. Deceit is all-pervasive. It encompasses the methods used to procure euthanasia drugs, the planning of the death itself, and the disposal of the body and associated paperwork. Prior to death, doctors admitted to fabricating symptoms in order to create a plausible clinical basis for the prescription or administration of escalating dosages of drugs. In other cases, drugs were simply stolen, or hoarded and redistributed by health carers, patients, and even care organizations. Lying on death certificates, and on cremation certificates, was universal. . . .

The Need to Minimize Harm

It is ironic that while debate continues over whether law could ever make the practice of euthanasia safe, professional medical bodies continue to ignore the illicit practice of PAS/AVE by their members. Similarly, while entire careers are devoted to dissecting the Dutch data, euthanasia opponents rarely acknowledge what is going on in their own back yard. There is a tendency among opponents to discount the social harm caused by illicit euthanasia, when compared to the anticipated harm that would be caused if euthanasia were legalized. The assumption is that while legalizing euthanasia introduces the risks of a "slippery slope" towards non-consensual killing, illicit euthanasia merely involves the deaths of those who would die anyway under a legalized regime. It follows that illicit euthanasia causes *less harm* than legalized euthanasia. . . . This ignores the fact that what is absent in the euthanasia underground is any sort of quality assurance mechanism. Although interviewees appreciated the complex meanings of suicide talk, their accounts of first-hand involvement demonstrate that patients died without having received assessment for depression or dementia, without adequate counseling or palliative care, and without specialist assessments as to prognosis and treatment alternatives. Advocates and opponents of euthanasia share common ground in wanting to prevent deaths under these circumstances.

The approach to euthanasia policy that I advocate in this paper distinguishes between personal morality (one's personal views about the morality of euthanasia) and social policy. Since the rightness or wrongness of assisted dying in all its forms, and in different circumstances, remains a matter of fundamental dispute, social policy ought to be about more than trying to impose one's own view of what is right upon everyone else. . . .

One is forced to confront the detriments of the current policy of prohibition, and to compare these against the detriments of alternative policies. The assumption behind legalization as a policy is that a statutory regime provides the opportunity for law to re-regulate euthanasia and to protect patients through the safeguards that would be pre-conditions to lawful assistance. The policy equation requires one to weigh the potential for the abuse of sick and vulnerable patients, together with the possible corrosion of worthy community values, in an environment where the law permits assistance-in-dying, against the harm that illicit practices themselves represent, as well as the suffering of those who are currently unable to obtain adequate relief or to mobilize covert assistance. . . .

Assisted Death Safeguards

Opponents of euthanasia often try to advance their case by shooting holes in the safeguards that advocates of legalization would like to see included in any statutory protocol or decision-making process. . . . Opponents argue that safeguards would fail in their purpose because they are inherently malleable, vague or open to abuse. . . .

As [Arthur] Caplan and colleagues recognize, the architects of statutory safeguards or guidelines can give no guarantees against abuse. Medicine is shot through with clinical scenarios that require the exercise of a discretion: PAS/AVE is hardly novel. The decision to withdraw life-support when further treatment is futile (a lawful practice) is not value free, and nor are the decisions that would be steps and safeguards in any PAS/AVE protocol. However, the fact that concepts like unbearable suffering, terminal illness, depression or competency have fuzzy edges does not mean that they provide no constraints on behaviour. . . .

Many Doctors Will Comply with Guidelines

A second argument against the efficacy of safeguards for the proposed practice of lawful PAS/AVE is that doctors would not follow them anyway, because they are a nuisance, too cumbersome, potentially incriminating, or intrude unduly into the privacy of the doctor/patient relationship. "[I]f the practice of physician-assisted suicide is already widespread but currently carried out with legal impunity, why should we expect doctors who now freely break the law to pay attention to new regulations any more than they do to the present one?" asks Callahan. "If they feel they can violate a long-standing moral prohibition in medicine to assist a suicide, why should we expect a sudden new respect for medical morality in the future?". . .

As a harm minimization strategy, legalization depends on the assumption that legalizing assisted death will prompt doctors to channel their activities back within statutory boundaries. But even partial compliance will be a benefit—the more influence a statutory protocol has on underground practices, the safer patients will be. . . .

The Netherlands is an easy target for those concerned about the efficacy of safeguards, since its policy of legalization

How Legal Euthanasia Is Regulated

The only four places that today *openly* and *legally,* authorize active assistance in dying of patients, are:

1. **Oregon** (since 1997, physician-assisted suicide only);

2. **Switzerland** (1941, physician and non-physician assisted suicide only);

3. **Belgium** (2002, permits 'euthanasia' but does not define the method;

4. **Netherlands** (voluntary euthanasia and physician-assisted suicide lawful since April 2002 but permitted by the courts since 1984).

Two doctors must be involved in Oregon, Belgium, and the Netherlands, plus a psychologist if there are doubts about the patient's competency. But that is not stipulated in Switzerland....

The Netherlands permits voluntary euthanasia as well as physician-assisted suicide, while both Oregon and Switzerland bar death by injection.

Belgian law speaks only of 'euthanasia' being available under certain conditions, 'Assisted suicide' appears to be a term that Belgians are not familiar with....

Derek Humphry, "Tread Carefully When You Help to Die: Assisted Suicide Laws Around the World," Assisted Suicide, March 1, 2005. www.assistedsuicide.org.

has brought a level of transparency that is absent in countries where PAS/AVE remains illegal. As [John] Griffiths points out, for all the criticism of non-compliance with safeguards under the Dutch PAS/AVE regime, the reporting rate for euthanasia in other countries, is zero. Curiously, euthanasia opponents seem more concerned about statistics in the Netherlands, than with the implications of underground euthanasia in their home countries. . . .

While intention is indeed a slippery thing, the growing body of survey evidence suggests that it is no longer reasonable to argue that doctors never break the law. No one denies that only a statistical minority of doctors are involved in PAS/AVE in the United States, Britain, and other prohibitionist countries: the same could be said of the Netherlands. . . . If these practices really do amount to the murder of vulnerable patients, why aren't euthanasia opponents screaming at the top of their lungs? Only a small minority of patients in the Netherlands die through PAS/AVE, and yet a whole industry has grown up in response to concerns about their welfare. To recognize the reality of illicit PAS/AVE, however, requires opponents to recognize that the Dutch did not invent euthanasia, and to temper their criticism of Dutch efforts to control these very risky practices. Whatever the shortcomings of Dutch policy, it is likely to be very difficult to introduce safeguards so long as assisted suicide remains illegal.

Legal Assisted Death Could Improve Palliative Care

A third argument against the legalization of euthanasia is that no statutory protocol could ever be safe if it operates against a backdrop of inadequate health care or symptom relief. . . . No patient, it seems, could safely be exposed to a euthanasia protocol in the absence of clear evidence that they were receiving world's best care. . . .

Opposition to assisted death becomes more troubling in the absence of the political will to actually fund the strategies needed to improve levels of care. What, exactly, is rational or compassionate about opposing the legalization of assisted death because it will ease the passing of those unable to access adequate care? Why should patients suffer, waiting for an "ideal" standard of care that—given spending priorities—may never arrive? . . .

Another factor to bear in mind is the possibility that removing bans on PAS/AVE may do more to mobilize the availability of palliative care services than the status quo. . . .

The Slippery Slope vs. Current Social Harm

Perhaps the most pervasive challenge to legalization as a harm reduction strategy is the argument that a euthanasia law will expose to risk a class of people who are not currently at risk while euthanasia remains illegal. This concern is typically expressed in the language of the "slippery slope." Slippery slope arguments highlight the anticipated negative consequences of legalization (such as the failure of safeguards), or go further and argue that legalization is a distinct link in a causal chain leading to a dark future.

Factoring in the merits of slippery slope arguments into a policy assessment is difficult, since these arguments are often best understood as "expressions of allegiance to the moral superiority of the status quo position," rather than careful assessments of likely consequences. Two points should be borne in mind. Firstly, as [Govert] den Hartogh notes, "the status quo has its moral costs as well." Slippery slope theorists overwhelmingly emphasize the anticipated social costs of legalization, while ignoring the social costs of prohibition. Underground euthanasia undermines a key assumption of slippery slope theories: that if PAS/AVE is legalized, bad things will *start to happen.* The fact is, harmful, unsafe things are already happening. Covert PAS/AVE is thus an unwelcome challenge to slippery slope theorists.

One of the few opponents of euthanasia to acknowledge the practice of illicit PAS/AVE, is [M.] Somerville. . . .

Somerville argues that the symbolism of law's prohibition has great value at the macro or societal level, even if in rare instances doctors are not prosecuted or are dealt with leniently. She also believes that the fear of prosecution is an enormous safeguard for patients. To some extent this may be true. But fear of prosecution also contributes to "botched attempts," it inhibits discussion, "second opinions" and other safeguards, leads to the fudging of medical charts and creates an all-permeating culture of deception. These costs also need to be weighed in the balance. . . .

Personal Beliefs vs. Public Benefit

I began this paper by pointing to the growing body of survey evidence that demonstrates the illicit practice of PAS/AVE by anything between four to more than ten percent of doctors. . . . If all underground deaths were well considered and went smoothly, one might better justify the decision to ignore illicit PAS/AVE as just another example of a "victimless crime." The true nature of these underground practices, however, adds a worrying new dimension to the statistics. We need a new debate: one that takes account of underground PAS/AVE, and is honest about the risks that prohibition, as well as legalization, pose for patients.

Opponents of legalization are quick to point out that just because illicit euthanasia occurs, or just because a dying person "consents" to being killed, does not provide a good reason for legalizing it. There may well be, according to opponents, an underground in pedophilia; the laws against rape are regularly broken, and a person may consent to bestiality and to sniffing cocaine. But since none of these things should be legalized, there is no good reason for considering the legalization of euthanasia either.

This argument is only persuasive if one cannot draw any moral distinction between *anything* that is illegal, whether it be sexual relations with children, assisting the death of a dying person, drinking alcohol (at times when this was illegal) or smoking cannabis. . . . There will always be those who believe that euthanasia should never be legalized because it amounts to intentional killing. For others, however, assisting the death of a terminally ill person is *contingently,* rather than inherently, wrong. Advocates argue that what can make it morally permissible is the compassionate motivation of the health care worker in bringing relief to an exhausted, tormented patient, and the importance of personal autonomy, which gives weight to a person's own perceptions of dignity. . . .

In areas where there is fundamental disagreement about whether or not something is inherently wrong, it is prudent for policy makers to distinguish between their personal moral beliefs, and broader questions of public benefit. The challenge for policy makers is to carefully assess the consequences of prohibition against the risks, benefits and detriments of alternative approaches. Sensible debate about harm minimization can as easily be hijacked by those who cannot see the harmful consequences of prohibiting PAS/AVE, as by those who cannot admit the possibility that laws legalizing PAS/AVE may have a lasting impact on social attitudes toward dying.

"I think it's realistic to hope for a future in which nobody has to die alone and nobody has to die with their pain untreated."

Improved End-of-Life Care Would Make Assisted Suicide Unnecessary

Ira Byock, interviewed by Steve Gordon

In the following viewpoint journalist Steve Gordon interviews Ira Byock, who is the director of palliative medicine at Dartmouth-Hitchcock Medical Center in New Hampshire and the author of several books, including Dying Well. *Byock argues that both sides of the debate on assisted suicide are wrong, and that the public's primary concern should be improving end-of-life care for dying patients. He contends that if patients' suffering could be adequately addressed, no one would request a physician's aid in dying.*

As you read, consider the following questions:

1. What does Byock cite as a bedrock issue for end-of-life care?
2. What is Byock's view on suicide versus assisted suicide?
3. What is Byock's concern if doctors are involved with assisted suicide?

From his small office in the newest part of the Dartmouth-Hitchcock Medical Center, Ira Byock hopes to bring about something of a revolution. He wants to dramatically improve the care provided to people who are very old or very sick and dying. . . .

[His] vision . . . is to bring the principles of good palliative care—effective pain management, for instance, and support for patients and families that goes beyond diagnosis and treatment—to virtually all aspects of medical care.

"I think it's realistic to hope for a future in which nobody has to die alone and nobody has to die with their pain untreated," he wrote in his 1997 book *Dying Well: Peace and Possibilities at the End of Life.*

What is needed to make that happen, among other changes, is better physician education, and more active support from the individuals and institutions in patients' communities, Byock said.

What is not needed, in his opinion, is a law legalizing physician-assisted suicide. . . .

What follows is an edited transcript of an interview with Byock. . . .

Both Pro and Con Positions Off-Track

Ira Byock: *If we were to legalize physician-assisted suicide in Vermont or New Hampshire or anywhere, tomorrow, the next day we would still have problems of medical education which would remain inadequate; with the treatment of pain, which would remain inadequate; with the use of advance directives, which would remain inadequate; with the lack of community support, . . . with the incredible short-staffing in our nursing homes and home health.*

I used to be an ardent combatant for the con side, for the opposed side of the physician-assisted suicide debate. My stance now is that both sides are wrong. To the people who are promoting physician-assisted suicide, what I want to know is, what are you going to do *after* you win? Are you going to help us to work on the bedrock issue that there're not enough nurse's aides in our nursing homes to help people who want to eat but can't? Or are you going to perhaps work to expand the assisted-suicide law so that people who are unable to take the pills themselves can still make use of this "hastened death"? I think we are deluding ourselves by thinking that this is the main issue that we need to discuss.

Steve Gordon: What do you say to the other side?

I'll tell you, the religious groups that have opposed (it), and the right-to-life groups, should be ashamed of themselves. Because they have only told us what they're against. And I'm sorry, but that's a half a stance. They've yet to tell us or to show us what they're really for. In addition to being against physician-assisted suicide, where are you when studies are published that show that elderly nursing home residents are starving because there are not enough nurse's aides to help them eat? Where are you when the (federal) DEA cracks down on the adequate treatment of pain, the adequate prescribing of pain medications?

You mean making it harder to take care of people's pain?

Right. Where are you on these bedrock issues about how we care for people? They have been remarkably silent in telling us what they're for, and more importantly, in developing programs to show us what enlightened volunteer and community support looks like for the people who, absent that support, look at their future and see only suffering or suicide. If that's the Sophie's choice that people are presented with, then the choice of a seriously ill person to end their life might be entirely rational. But if so, I would submit, it's all the more tragic.

Assisted Suicide Not the Answer

You described the physician-assisted suicide debate recently as a distraction. The point you seem to be making is that it is a distraction from the more important discussions that should be taking place. But is there room for both? Let's say that the people who are in favor of physician-assisted suicide had an answer for your question—What are you going to do the next day?—and your ideal for improving the choices were really (carried out). You would still have people who were close to death, and in great pain that was hard to manage . . .

So are we having an abstract conversation now? Are we having a philosophical conversation? Because, in fact, I don't know how many people there would be.

I'm just wondering whether even in your vision of a better world for people facing serious illness and death, there might still be room for somebody to decide, I just don't want to go through the next two weeks or whatever it might be of intense pain. I'd like to end my life earlier. Is there potentially room for that?

I think that's a question that voters and society need to decide. I have other priorities to work on rather than that. And I believe that physicians will continue to have more than enough challenges in taking really good care of patients to stay focused there.

I think suicide and physician-assisted suicide are two very different things. I am not going to institute a psychiatric hold on somebody with far advanced illness who has hoarded pills and decides to end their life. But I don't think it's the role of a physician, certainly not my role, to assist them in pre-empting death.

In fact, most people who come to me and say (they are) interested in having lethal prescriptions are currently taking

Responding to Suffering

When all things are considered, the arguments in favor of continued prohibition of physician-assisted suicide are not particularly compelling. . . .

Those of us opposed to physician-assisted suicide would do well to focus our efforts on helping others discover the meaning and hope that are possible in life, even in the midst of suffering. . . . If we were to do a better job of responding to suffering individuals in a loving, caring manner, physician-assisted suicide would in all likelihood be an option rarely, if ever, chosen.

Daniel E. Lee, Hastings Center Report, January/February 2003.

medications to prolong their life, and have lots of ways that they could end their life without my help. What they're asking for is my almost priestly blessing that they are as helpless and hopeless as they feel. And in fact, therapeutically, I believe my role is to help them to discover some hope and some sense of value in whatever life is remaining.

Whether it's months, weeks, days or hours.

Exactly. Yes. Now, you said, well, they don't want to go through the last two weeks of life. Well, you know, the Oregon law won't help you in that situation. The bill that's going to be introduced in Vermont wouldn't help in that situation, because there's a two-week waiting period between the two (doctor) visits. But many people who want to do that could die more quickly simply by stopping the medications they're currently taking and perhaps by not forcing themselves to eat when they're not hungry and drink when they're not thirsty. They already have the control that they're seeking. It's not the right issue.

Better Solutions to End-of-Life Challenges

If you could pull the Vermont law[1] that's being discussed now right off the table, and replace it with your idea of what would be a better thing for a state government to do, is there anything that comes to mind?

I hope to be active in the discussion in Vermont. I am going to avoid being an opponent of the physician-assisted suicide law. What I would like to challenge its supporters to do—as well as the medical profession in Vermont, the legislature, the governor—is to also introduce a bill that would require at least 100 hours of medical training related to components of palliative care within the required education of every medical student trained in Vermont as a condition for graduating from medical school.

We currently require 170 to 200 hours of obstetrics training for every medical student prior to graduation, and yet very few students ever go on to deliver babies in practice, and every single one who does has taken a separate post-graduate residency in obstetrics or in family practice. The majority of physicians, whatever their discipline, end up helping to care for people through the last year of their lives.

Secondly, I think that bill should require that the state board of medical examiners test and certify that each physician demonstrate basic skills and knowledge of pain assessment and management as a condition for receiving or renewing a medical license. Because these are core skills of medicine. The fact that we are not teaching them and that demonstrably many physicians in practice don't have these basic skills is not OK. It would be as if the FAA [Federal Aviation Administration] were saying pilots have to take off and fly, but being able to land is optional.

1. The Vermont Death with Dignity Act, H.168, was not voted out of the Vermont House Human Services Committee as of the end of the 2004–2005 legislative session.

I think the proposals to legalize assisted-suicide, from my perspective, would be better constructed if they left the role of the physician solely in certifying that a patient has a qualifying condition. And otherwise left medicine out of the process. If a law were to be passed in this regard, the physician, just like we do with any number of other things, would say, yes, Joe has advanced cancer, or yes, Joe has far advanced congestive heart failure, or ALS [Amyotrophic Lateral Sclerosis, also known as Lou Gehrig's disease] or whatever. And then, under whatever the proposed law would be, Joe, having that certification, and having met any other requirements, could go to the pharmacy and get the medicine without a prescription. The authority came from the legislature to the patient.

So if you as a physician certified that I was terminally ill, I could, with the authority of the legislature, get a lethal dose of something from a pharmacy.

These are, after all, one-size-fits-all prescriptions. You don't need a physician's prescribing expertise to do this.

My worry is that when you legalize something like this, it becomes routinized. And then, a lot of different types of suffering will look like they fit into this category. I think as a culture, and I can certainly say as a medical culture, we are not mature enough to be given authority to end people's life by intention. It's like giving a 3-year-old a hammer. The entire world starts to look like a nail.

There are a lot of types of suffering that we physicians address which are very difficult to control and help people with. And we struggle with the people. That is the root of the word compassion, to suffer with. And I submit that if we begin as a society and culture to make pre-empting death seem wholesome, we will find that it is a solution to many problems that we encounter every day. That's why, speaking as a physician, somebody who is proud to be a physician, I don't think it's a good thing for us to go down this path. And if society is hell-bent to legalize assisted suicide, then I hope the legislature gives that authority to somebody else.

> *"Physician-assisted death should represent a small but critical piece of a larger puzzle of improving end-of-life care for all dying persons."*

Improved End-of-Life Care Would Not Make Assisted Suicide Unnecessary

Timothy E. Quill and Margaret P. Battin

Timothy E. Quill and Margaret P. Battin make a case in the following viewpoint for physician-assisted suicide as a necessary part of compassionate end-of-life care. Even the best hospice programs, argue the authors, cannot relieve suffering for a small percentage of patients. For some of these people, simply knowing that they can receive aid in dying should they request it makes the suffering bearable. For others, the pain will be too great, and they will choose physician-assisted suicide as the only way to relieve their misery. Timothy Quill is a professor of medicine at the University of Rochester School of Medicine and Dentistry. He has authored and edited numerous books on end-of-life issues. Margaret Battin is a professor of philosophy in the division of medical ethics at the University of Utah and is also a prolific author on ethics and dying.

As you read, consider the following questions:

Timothy E. Quill, MD., and Margaret P. Battin, Ph. D., eds., *Physician-Assisted Dying: The Case for Palliative Care and Patient Choice.* Baltimore: Johns Hopkins University Press, 2004. Copyright © 2004 by Johns Hopkins University Press. Reproduced by permission.

1. What types of suffering other than physical do the authors list?

2. How many patients who explore the option of assisted suicide actually die that way, according to Quill and Battin?

3. When a conflict of values exists, what order of priority do the authors recommend?

To understand the role of physician-assisted death as a last-resort option restricted to dying patients for whom palliative care or hospice has become ineffective or unacceptable, one must understand how frequently and under what circumstances that occurs. If all such cases are the result of inadequately delivered palliative care, then the best answer would be to improve the standard of care and make the problem disappear. Most experts in pain management believe that 95 to 98 percent of pain among those who are terminally ill can be adequately relieved using modern pain management, which is a remarkable track record—unless you are unfortunate enough to be in the 2 to 5 percent for whom it is unsuccessful. However, among hospice patients who were asked about their pain level one week before their death, 5 to 35 percent rated their pain as "severe" or "unbearable." An additional 25 percent reported their shortness of breath to be "unbearable" one week before death. This says nothing of the physical symptoms that are harder to relieve, such as nausea, vomiting, confusion, and open wounds, including pressure sores, which many patients experience.

Suffering at the End of Life

Of course, dying patients do not have the luxury of cleanly separating their physical suffering from their psychological, spiritual, and existential suffering. These common physical symptoms are only part of the puzzle of suffering at the end of life. We now know from Oregon that many patients who

A View of Human Dignity

Dignity is an essentially human element in quality of life and its loss is for many the ultimate humiliation. There are few who find it easy to contemplate the irreversible loss of control over mental and/or bodily functions which can be a consequence of the ravages of disease, particularly with advancing age.

There is far more to human life than a beating heart, the drawing of breath, or the reaction of nerves to a stimulus. Life encompasses self-awareness, the ability to communicate with others and to pursue meaningful activities. In that sense, to be alive is to have a conscious identity, to be a person. When life no longer has that quality, but has been permanently replaced by a burdensome existence it makes little sense to speak of a "right" to life. It becomes an obligation if we can under no circumstances surrender it.

South Australian Voluntary Euthanasia Society,
"The Moral Case," Handbook of the South
Australian Voluntary Euthanasia Society, 1998.

contemplate ending their own lives under the Death with Dignity Act have these physical symptoms but also report that tiredness with the process of dying, feeling out of control, and lack of meaning are frequently the most important reasons for requesting a hastened death. We also know that dying patients who consider hastening their deaths have trouble envisioning a meaningful future and that they score high on hopelessness scale. Some patients who consider ending their lives under these circumstances are clinically depressed, but others are not, and none of these patients evaluated by a psychiatrist under the Death with Dignity Act was found to have distorted judgment from depression. The reality faced by dying patients and their families in terms of suffering, even in the best of hospice programs, is much more complex than is ordinarily acknowledged. Eighty-five percent of the 171 patients who dies with the assistance of a physician under the Oregon law were simultaneously enrolled in a hospice program, so for them the dichotomous choice "palliative care or physician-assisted death" was clearly insufficient.

Illegal Options

What are the effects of current prohibitions against access to physician-assisted death? Practices of last resort, such as physician-assisted suicide, that are illegal outside of Oregon are difficult to study because clinicians and family members could be criminally liable if they openly admitted to having participated. In reality, U.S. policy outside of Oregon would more aptly be characterized as "don't ask, don't tell," as the medical and legal professions have shown little enthusiasm about actively pursuing such cases through either legal or professional channels. Empirical studies on the illegal practice of physician-assisted death suggest that it accounts for a small percentage of overall deaths everywhere it has been studied, although in select populations, such as AIDS patients in San Francisco before the introduction of protease inhibitors, the practice may have accounted for almost 50 percent of deaths.

If the "don't ask, don't tell" policy is working reasonably well, why not just leave it alone? The answer to this question is that it is not working well, for several reasons. First, access to the option of physician-assisted death is uneven and unpredictable, probably depending more on the physician's values and willingness to take a risk on the patient's behalf than on the patient's values and clinical circumstances. Second, explicit conversation carries some risk, so patients, families, and their medical providers may communicate tacitly, with a wink and a nod instead of forthright conversation, with the concomitant potential for dangerous, possibly lethal misunderstandings in this delicate area. Third, there would be no guarantee of adequate palliative care being in place before last-resort options were considered, so it would be more likely that a hastened death would be implemented in the absence of standard of care for the dying. Empirical data potentially comparing open, legal access to physician-assisted death to secret, illegal practice in many localities—including the United States outside of Oregon, Australia, Belgium, Denmark, Italy, the Netherlands, Sweden, and Switzerland—are now becoming available. Of course, empirical data will not resolve the associated ethical or religious questions, but they will help to resolve some of the more secular issues around relative harm and benefit from legalization of assisted dying.

Legal Last Resort Options

One of the positive outcomes of the debate about legalization of physician-assisted suicide is that other last-resort options have been considered—and, in some cases, legitimated. There is growing acknowledgment that some patients experience unacceptable levels of suffering toward the end of their terminal illness, even though they are receiving state-of-the-art palliative care, and that some of these patients are capable of making rational decisions to hasten death (that is, they are not all clinically depressed or delirious). For example, patients are allowed to discontinue life support as part of their right to bodily integrity, even when their desire is to die sooner rather than later. Patients who may have been taking a lesser amount of opioids for their pain so as to maintain alertness at one point in their illness may at a latter stage request or accept more risk of sedation to achieve better pain relief as death approaches.

Two new options of last resort, voluntarily stopping eating and drinking and terminal sedation, have now been recognized as legally acceptable and are beginning to be more completely discussed from ethical and religious perspectives. Voluntary cessation of eating and drinking involves a conscious choice to hasten death by a severely ill person who is still capable of eating and drinking. It is viewed ethically by many as a variant of the right to refuse treatment, as part of an individual's right to bodily integrity. Terminal sedation, which involves sedating the patient to unconsciousness (to allow an escape from suffering) and then withholding or withdrawing hydration and nutrition, is generally reserved for imminently dying patients whose physical suffering is severe and otherwise unrelievable. Sedation to the point of unconsciousness is viewed by many as aggressive symptom palliation with the intent to relieve suffering (therefore consistent with the doctrine of double effect), and the withdrawal of life-sustaining nutrition and hydration as part of the right to bodily integrity. Of course, either or both of these acts could be used intentionally to hasten a wished-for death and therefore be consistent with physician-assisted suicide or even voluntary active euthanasia, which makes these practices problematic for some clinicians and patients even if they are legally permissible.

Becoming more explicit about the acceptability of these last-resort practices has been an important contribution to enhancing end-of-life options for many patients. It acknowledges that tough cases of unacceptable suffering exist, and it reinforces clinicians' obligation to respond to suffering. Additional options can be offered to patients who otherwise would have no acceptable possibilities. For patients who are morally opposed to physician-assisted suicide yet nonetheless find themselves in intolerable clinical circumstances, these alternative last-resort practices may provide acceptable options to allow them to live (and die) on their own terms.

Doctors Can Alleviate Fear

The possibility of a predictable escape from suffering if it becomes overwhelming is important to many patients, especially those who have witnessed bad deaths in loved ones toward whom the medical profession was unable or unwilling to be responsive. This fear is probably the driving force behind the desire for legalization of physician-assisted suicide. . . . Having this conversation relatively early on in a patient's potentially terminal illness lets the patient know that the clinician is not afraid of the dying process and provides opportunity to educate the patient about all the advances palliative care has made in terms of addressing pain and other symptoms. Some patients, however, may push the family or their medical providers further by asking questions like, "If my pain becomes intolerable, will you help me die?" Sometimes this will be a general exploration of the extent of commitment not to abandon, but at other times it may include explicit exploration of what last-resort options can be supported. We know from the Netherlands that only about one in nine patients who explore the option of physician-assisted dying actually dies in this way. Patients who know that their doctor is a committed medical partner, and that acceptable medical options are available to address their fears and concerns, will then have the freedom to spend their time and energy on other more vital matters as they are dying. Those without this knowledge and commitment are left to wonder fearfully how their final weeks and months might unfold.

Usually, even when a physician has promised to be responsive in helping a patient die, careful delivery of palliative care and then hospice is sufficient to facilitate an acceptable, if not always ideal, death. Anecdotal evidence suggests that many patients try to protect their physicians and family members from legal risk even at the cost of their own suffering. Yet there will be cases in which suffering becomes severe and unacceptable, and a patient becomes ready to die sooner rather than later and is willing to ask for help. All such patients should be assessed in a similar way to ensure that all reasonable palliative care options have been considered, no matter which last-resort options are also being contemplated. Have pain or other physical symptoms been adequately addressed? Has the patient become depressed in a way that is distorting his judgment? Has a family or spiritual crisis developed? If a careful assessment finds none of those elements present, is the request genuine and in proportion to the degree of the patient's suffering? Here the safeguards and second opinions of an open process become invaluable. Whether the physician is considering stopping life support (legal) or providing medication that can be taken as an overdose (in the United States, illegal outside of Oregon), he or she must recognize that the patient is likely to die as a result of this decision, so it should be approached with the utmost care and caution. As always, safeguards for any of these last-resort practices must balance invasiveness and safety.

Choosing a Method of Death

Once the assessment has been carried out to ensure that all reasonable palliative care alternatives that the patient is willing to accept have been considered and that the patient is clear about the request and the implications for him- or herself and the family, then a decision must be made about methods. The method chosen should be the least invasive and risky for the particular patient, taking into account his or her values and clinical circumstances. If the method includes physician participation, the physician's values must be taken into account, as well. If a physician is unwilling to participate in a legally accepted option for which the patient otherwise would qualify and which he or she desires, then the physician is obligated to offer to transfer the patient's care to a qualified physician with different views and values. The physician must not entrap patients by seeming to promise a physician-assisted death but then reneging on this promise. If a physician is aware of all the last-resort options and is opposed to granting a request for assisted suicide by a particular patient, the physician might explore those options that he or she *can* support to see whether common ground can be found. Clearly, physicians should attempt to extend themselves to remain responsive to such suffering patients and their families, but that should not include violating fundamental personal moral values for either the physician or the patient. On the other hand, it is imperative that we now recognize that the patient's fundamental moral values may include physician-assisted suicide and that this option, for those who are dying, should be part of recognized law.

The Importance of Physician-Assisted Death

Although issues around legal access to physician-assisted death remain complex and controversial, we support the following conclusions. . .:

- Excellent palliative care must be the standard of care for those who are severely ill and dying. It can address, and sufficiently relieve, most but not all suffering that accompanies the dying process.

- Strong philosophical, ethical, and religious principles— especially autonomy, mercy, and nonabandonment— support access to physician-assisted death as a last resort for those circumstances in which suffering becomes intolerable to a dying patient who has access to palliative care.

- When conflicts about values exist in end-of-life care, it is the patient's values that count most (it is his or her death, after all), followed by those of the family (who have to make sense of the decisions that have been made) and then those of the health care providers (if it involves their participation). In areas in which there is no societal consensus about permissible versus impermissible actions, patients, families, and their health care providers should be given as much lee-way and support as possible as they face these difficult decisions. . . .

- Although relatively few patients actually receive physician-assisted suicide, knowing about it as a possibility (as well as knowing about other last-resort options, such as stopping life-sustaining therapy, terminal sedation, or stopping eating and drinking) is important to many who fear hard death and need to know that they could have some choice in the process.

- Physician-assisted suicide should be viewed in the context of other last-resort options in which death is hastened, including discontinuing life-sustaining therapy, terminal sedation, and cessation of eating and drinking. The challenge clinically is to respond appropriately to the particular patient's clinical circumstances in light of his or her values and those of the family and the physician. . . .

In our opinion, physician-assisted death should represent a small but critical piece of a larger puzzle of improving end-of-life care for all dying persons. In the absence of universal medical insurance coverage, the first step in working with patients who are nearing death, whether or not they are exploring the possibility of an assisted death, is to ensure they have access to the best medical care possible. We must all join together in working toward improvements in palliative care and hospice, in hopes of making them accessible to all seriously ill patients. . . .

The Choice of How to Die

Vulnerable patients are asking us to listen to their requests with an open mind and heart and to keep their values and priorities at the center of the decision-making process. After all, this is a process driven by the experiences of dying patients and their families. Patients who begin to experience a bad death need access to experienced palliative care consultants who can make sure everything possible is being done to address their suffering, and make it tolerable. They need committed medical partners who will help them explore all potential alternatives but also address the reality that sometimes death is not the enemy. People who are terminally ill do not have a choice about whether to die, but they are asking for some choice and control over *how* they die. For many, potential access to a physician-assisted death allows reassurance that there could be an escape that they may never need. For a few who reach a point at which continued living becomes unacceptable and personhood is rapidly disintegrating, open access to a physician-assisted death can be vital to maintaining dignity and meaning at death.

> "What I cannot stomach is the idea of applying to the state for a licence, to be issued upon the determination of an appointed regulatory body, to kill or be killed."

Legalizing Assisted Suicide Would Make Killing Too Easy

Matthew Parris

In the following viewpoint, British journalist and politician Matthew Parris describes his primary reason for opposing legal euthanasia: It would make killing too easy. If euthanasia were legal, one would merely have to appeal to a governmental advisory board for permission to kill an ailing friend or relative. Parris believes that mercy killing should be made as hard as possible in order to preserve respect for human life, and so supports the law against euthanasia. Forcing people to risk prison for aiding in someone's death is an appropriate test of their love and respect, he contends. Parris is a former Minister of Parliament in the United Kingdom, a columnist for the Times *and the* Spectator *in the United Kingdom, and the author of numerous books, including* Chance Witness: An Outsider's Life in Politics.

As you read, consider the following questions:

1. What situation caused the author to reconsider his position on legal euthanasia?

2. According to Parris, what two ways could the government choose to reform the laws on euthanasia?

3. When does the author say the need for euthanasia arises?

Sometimes one's creed points logically where one is intuitively reluctant to go. The flesh is willing but the spirit is weak. Item: we should not give money to women begging with babies as this only encourages them. Item: this is a beggar and she is carrying a baby. Conclusion: . . . er . . . fumble in pockets for change. (She just looked so wretched.)

One settles such conflicts by following a hunch. This is not necessarily the triumph of unreason. We should never question the primacy of reason, but we cannot always be sure what reason dictates. Sometimes the heart may guess early at reasons which the brain proves slower to recognise. Sound argument should be paramount, yes, but sometimes intuition is early warning of an argument that is not as sound as it seems.

Libertarian View of Legalizing Euthanasia

And so it happened that, libertarian to my boots, I thought I would be in favour of what euthanasia campaigners call the Right to Die until this week BBC 1's *The Morning Show* asked me to do a turn on their sofa to discuss Mr Reginald Crew's plan (he is now the late Mr Reginald Crew) to travel to Switzerland where he could be assisted to kill himself. Mr Crew, who was 74, had been suffering for four years from motor neurone disease; there was no cure, his deterioration was remorseless, and life had become (he said) no longer worth living.

An action which causes another person's death, even at his request, is unlawful in Switzerland as it is here [in the United Kingdom], but the Swiss have been more flexible in their prosecution policy and tend to turn a blind eye to the work of reputable and humane organisations such as Dignitas, the

Asay. © 1996 by Chuck Asay. Reproduced by permission of Chuck Asay and Creators Syndicate, Inc.

group that assisted Mr Crew by giving him poison to drink through a straw. Though his impunity in Switzerland was assured, it is not clear to me that this would have been a crime even here in Britain where we adhere as unbendingly as we can to the distinction between failing to resuscitate or prolong life, which is not usually a crime, and actively taking life, which usually is. This is a blurred and difficult frontier to police; prosecution is not the invariable rule, conviction does not always follow, and, if it does, sentences are usually lenient or even derisory. But the line is more or less held.

After agreeing to appear on *The Morning Show,* I sat down quietly and thought my libertarianism through. I knew intuitively that I admired Mr Crew and might well have done the same were I in his dilemma. But should he have had to go to Switzerland to face it?

It appeared to me that if we sought the kind of reform which would have assisted Mr Crew, two alternative means

Little Support for Euthanasia

Poll numbers in the United States are deceptive. Americans endorse a generalized and abstract right to die, but when pollsters ask questions relating to specific medical situations, public support declines. This is particularly true about voluntary active euthanasia, which Americans tend to tolerate but only when the patient is in unremitting pain and definitely terminally ill. In the final analysis, as bioethicist Ezekiel Emanuel argues, a "rule of thirds" dominates polling data regarding euthanasia: a third of Americans endorse legalization under a wide variety of circumstances, a third oppose it under any circumstances, and a third support it in isolated cases but oppose it under most circumstances. Support for either active euthanasia or physician-assisted suicide is neither strong nor deep. As the legal expert and anti-euthanasia warhorse Yale Kamisar declared in 2002, "it is much easier to sell the basic notion of assisted suicide than to sell a complex statute making the idea law." As regrettable as terminal sedation is, there is no evidence that public opinion prefers the alternative of changing professional standards and the law to authorize euthanasia, thus running the risk of any further erosion of society's respect for life.... "

Ian Dowbiggin, A Merciful End: The Euthanasia Movement in Modern America, 2003.

were available. We could make 'He asked me to' a defence to murder and have done with it, leaving judges and juries to determine case by case whether the accused really had satisfied himself that his victim was of sound mind and had formed the settled desire to have himself killed. But I saw, too, that, appealingly simple though (to a libertarian) this might be, it would never do. We cannot go around killing anyone who asks us to, however emphatically. The law would additionally want to know that the accused had made a reasonable attempt to satisfy himself that the victim's wish was well founded, that the accused had no ulterior motive, that he knew and understood the victim, that the victim had had all that was needful drawn to his attention, that. . . .

And I could see where, in Britain at least, the case for reform must tend: to the alternative of setting up a Euthanasia Commission composed of expert persons competent to decide applications for death. Killing people cannot be left to private initiative, the killer subsequently making the best defence he can to any putative murder charge. The proposal would have to be considered in advance by some sort of adjudicating body.

Euthanasia Is Killing

For let us be clear that killing people is what is under discussion. The late Mr Crew went to Switzerland to have poison poured down his throat. It is not quite honest to call this 'assisted suicide' and disingenuous to speak, as the euthanasia lobby do, of 'the right to die'. We already have the right to die. Suicide has not been a crime for some half a century. The need for euthanasia arises when the victim lacks the means or power to take his own life and can only request (on the instant or in advance by some sort of letter of intent) that someone else take his life. The euthanasia lobby wish to give that person the right to kill.

If you hand me a dagger and say, 'I am too weak to do it; here, plunge this between my ribs,' I take it you are asking me to kill you. If I comply, and am discovered, my discoverer will cry, 'You killed him!' and I will reply, 'Yes, but he asked me to.' What difference in principle is there between this and the less bloody alternative in which (say) you indicate a phial of poison and say, 'I am too weak to drink this; here, raise it to my lips and pour it down,' or, 'Inject me with this'? No question about it: you ask me to kill you.

I am not in principle against killing people. In a just war, in self-defence, as a means of preventing greater killing, or even (at times) in overwhelming sympathy for another's suffering, it is something we may contemplate. But to take another's life in peacetime is an enormous step, perhaps the most enormous. If there is anything which should not be done lightly or without anguish, this is it. For those who contemplate such an action, to be forced—at least to contemplate—losing the law's protection may not be an inappropriate hurdle to expect them to clear. I can think of worse tests of good faith than to ask that the killer love his victim enough to risk arrest for killing him.

I will kill myself if I ever have to, and I may. I would break the law and kill a friend if I ever had to—and face the consequences. But what I cannot stomach is the idea of applying to the state for a licence, to be issued upon the determination of an appointed regulatory body, to kill or be killed. If one man's Right to Die gives another the Right to Kill, and if the Right to Kill means giving the government the right to withdraw Permission to Live, then give me prison.

| "*Legalising euthanasia is premature when research evidence from the perspectives of those who desire euthanasia is scant.*"

Legalizing Physician-Assisted Suicide Is Premature

Yvonne Mak, Glyn Elwyn, and Ilora G. Finlay

Researchers Yvonne Mak, Glyn Elwyn, and Ilora G. Finlay argue in the following viewpoint that more studies should be done of patients who desire euthanasia before societies decide whether or not to legalize it. They contend that discovering the factors that lead to a wish for euthanasia could lead to viable approaches for addressing those issues. For example, if pain leads people to request euthanasia, better palliative care could be developed. Yvonne Mak is a medical officer at a hospice in Hong Kong; Glyn Elwyn is a professor at the University of Wales Swansea Clinical School; and Ilora Finlay is a professor of palliative medicine at the School of Medicine at the University of Wales.

As you read, consider the following question:

1. What do the authors say current debate about euthanasia has been founded upon?

2. What is a central controversy in the debate on euthanasia, according to the authors?

Yvonne Mak, Glyn Elwyn, and Ilora G. Finlay, "Patients' Voices Are Needed in Debates on Euthanasia," *British Medical Journal,* vol. 327, July 26, 2003, p. 213. Copyright © 2003 by the British Medical Association. Reproduced by permission of BMJ Publishing Group.

3. What do the authors encourage doctors to focus on rather than legal guidelines for euthanasia?

Medically assisted death is legal in a few countries, and discussion about legalisation is ongoing in many others. But legalisation may be premature when we still do not know why patients want euthanasia and whether better end of life care would change their views.

Countless debates have been held on euthanasia, but little research has been done into the experiences of patients who request it. Proponents portray all undignified death and opponents fear the potential dangers of legalising euthanasia, but the fundamental question is why patients want euthanasia. Current debates have been based on perspectives of medical professionals, academics, lawyers, politicians, and the public. Qualitative, experiential, and patient based research is needed to help capture the complexity of patients' subjective experiences and elucidate the influences and meanings that underpin their desire for death.

Arguments for and Against Legal Euthanasia

Justifications for legalisation of euthanasia have pivoted on unbearable suffering, respect for autonomy, and dignified death. Proponents argue, from the principles of compassion and self determination, that mentally competent patients with an incurable illness and intolerable suffering should be able to choose the manner and timing of their death. This view is gaining support within an increasingly secular society with an individualistic and utilitarian ethos.

Opponents highlight the potential dangers for patients, healthcare professionals, and society. Doctors should strive to relieve suffering, not end the life of the sufferer; the authority to terminate life would undermine their trustworthiness. Euthanasia is irreversible, yet the will to live often fluctuates widely over the course of a terminal illness.

Some opponents fear patients might feel obliged to request euthanasia to avoid being a burden, particularly as acts to end life already occur without the patients' explicit requests. Regulation of euthanasia cannot be securely enforced, which creates potential for abuse. Moral disintegration could occur when society views euthanasia as a cheaper and preferable option to providing care. Others believe that excellent palliative care obviates the need for euthanasia.

Defining Unbearable Suffering

A central controversy in euthanasia debates is the difficulty in defining and proving unbearable suffering. What are the dimensions of suffering experienced by patients who desire death? Are we paying adequate attention to diagnosing and relieving suffering, when the customary biomedical model of care has focused more on the disease than the patient? Are we comfortable and competent in communicating with people who are dying? Do we understand the genuine meaning of euthanasia requests? Is the topic of suffering emphasised in medical education and research? In effect, have we overlooked our patients' experience of suffering?

Most studies of euthanasia have been quantitative, focusing primarily on attitudes of healthcare professionals, relatives, and the public. The patients included in these studies were neither terminally ill nor currently desiring death [so] their attitudes in response to hypothetical scenarios might not indicate what they actually will want or do in the future. Nevertheless, these studies are important. Pain was cited as a major reason for requesting euthanasia; other influences included functional impairment, dependency, burden, social isolation, depression, hopelessness, and issues of control and autonomy.

A few recent qualitative studies have provided evidence about the perspectives of patients who desired death. Lavery and colleagues used a grounded theory approach to explore the origins of medically assisted death in HIV positive pa-

African Americans and Assisted Suicide

Given the general distrust of medical institutions and the medical profession and the belief that their lives are under-valued, African-Americans are likely to view the legalization of physician-assisted suicide (PAS) with suspicion. Rather than see it as an opportunity to exercise their autonomy at the end of life, African-Americans may sense that this is yet another way through which less valued African-American lives can be eliminated. . . .

The African-American experience with medicine also cau-tions against placing too much confidence in the ability of physicians and other healthcare providers to insure that pa-tient preferences are honored and respected. In the context of the patient-physician relationship, physicians have power. . . . In the face of the power inequities in this rela-tionship and the historical instances of misuse of power, African-Americans appreciate that making PAS available as an option for terminally ill patients does not necessarily empower those who have been disadvantaged. . . ..

Patricia A. King and Leslie E. Wolf, "Lessons for Physician Assisted Suicide from the African-American Experience," Physician-Assisted Suicide: Expanding the Debate, 1998.

tients. Two factors emerged: firstly, disintegration from symp-toms and functional loss and, secondly, loss of community, which they defined as diminishing opportunities to initiate and maintain close personal relationships, leading to a per-ceived loss of self. Johansen and colleagues interviewed pa-tients in a palliative care unit about their future wishes for eu-thanasia. Their views were hypothetical, ambivalent, and fluctuating, influenced by fears of future pain or a painful death, lack of quality of life, and lack of hope.

Two of us [Yvonne Mak] and [Glyn Elwyn] conducted a hermeneutic study with unstructured interviews to explore the meaning of desire for euthanasia in six patients with advanced cancer who had expressed a wish for euthanasia while receiving palliative care. We found five main themes: the reality of disease progression, perception of suffering, anticipation of a future worse than death, desires for good quality end of life care, and presence of care and connectedness. Thus the meaning of desire for euthanasia was not confined to physical and functional concerns but revealed hidden psychosocial and existential issues, understood within the context of the patients' whole life experiences.

The combination of disease progression and increasing suffering perceived along the illness journey gave rise to a sense of progressive disintegration of self or wholeness. This wholeness gradually diminished to the extent that patients could predict a negative future worse than death itself. Disintegration was likely to occur earlier if patients had unresolved life events, personality problems, or poor social support that threatened their sense of wholeness before they had cancer. The prospect of good quality end of life care and fulfilled needs helped alter their perceived reality and led to re-evaluation of their desire for death.

Caring for the Whole Person

These studies emphasise the importance of understanding the patients as a whole person in order to interpret the true meaning of requests for euthanasia. This includes their life experiences, perception and fears about their future, and yearnings for care and social connection to their community.

Legalising euthanasia is premature when research evidence from the perspectives of those who desire euthanasia is scant. More qualitative patient based studies are needed to broaden our understanding of patients. Inclusion of medical humanities, experiential learning, and reflective practice into medical education should help ensure doctors have better communication skills and attitudes. We must examine ways to improve care at all levels before we can eliminate the side effects of poor end of life care. The government should consider allocating adequate resources to reduce the burden of care as well as promoting education on death, and palliative care services should develop imaginative outreach services.

Rather than focusing on assessing the mental competence of patients requesting euthanasia or determining clear legal guidelines, doctors must acquire the skills for providing good end of life care. These include the ability to "connect" with patients, diagnose suffering, and understand patients' hidden agendas through in-depth exploration. This is especially important as the tenor of care influences patients' perception of hope and personal worth. There is much to ponder over the meaning of a euthanasia request before we have to consider its justification. The desire for euthanasia must not be taken at face value.

Periodical Bibliography

The following articles have been selected to supplement the diverse views presented in this chapter.

Gerard V. Bradley   "Death and the Law: Why the Government Has an Interest in Preserving Life," *World & I*, May 2003.

Ira Byock   "Both Sides Are Wrong in Suicide Debate," *Burlington Free Press*, February 7, 2005.

F. Michael Gloth   "Physician-Assisted Suicide: The Wrong Approach to End of Life Care," United States Conference of Catholic Bishops. www.nccbusc-c.org.

Herbert Hendin   "The Case Against Physician-Assisted Suicide: For the Right to End-of-Life Care," *Psychiatric Times*, February 1, 2004.

Herbert Hendin   "The Dutch Experience," *Issues in Law & Medicine*, March 22, 2002.

Johan Legemaate   "The Dutch Euthanasia Act and Related Issues," *Journal of Law and Medicine*, February 2004.

Linda Lyons   "Public Grapples with Legality, Morality of Euthanasia," *Gallup Poll Tuesday Briefing*, July 2004.

Betty Rollin   "Whose Life Is It, Anyway?" *O, The Oprah Magazine*, February 2003.

Lawrence Rudden   "Death and the Law," *World & I*, May 2003.

Wesley Sowers   "Physician Aid in Dying and the Role of Psychiatry," *Psychiatric Times*, January 1, 2004.

Laura Spinney   "Last Rights: If Someone Wants Help to End Their Life, Should the Law Stand in Their Way?" *New Scientist*, April 23, 2005.

OPPOSING
VIEWPOINTS®
SERIES

CHAPTER 3

Would Legalizing Voluntary Euthanasia Lead to Abuses?

Chapter Preface

Many people who oppose euthanasia do so not because they believe it is morally wrong but because they fear that legalizing the practice would lead to abuses. They reason that once the practice is allowed for patients who are terminally ill, in great pain, and who are near death, it becomes much more difficult to limit the practice to only these patients. Would the practice soon apply to those who endure extreme pain and suffering but who are not terminally ill? Or to those who primarily fear the loss of dignity but are not in pain? Opponents of euthanasia contend that there is no sure way to maintain adequate safeguards once legalization occurs. Furthermore, opponents fear that if these practices were legal, the disabled and the terminally ill may feel that because they could take advantage of an "early out," they should elect to do so in order to relieve the burden they are placing on their families. Opponents point to the Netherlands, where euthanasia is legal. According to them, in that nation nonvoluntary and involuntary euthanasia do at times occur, a prime illustration of the dangers of legalization. The contention that legalizing euthanasia for the terminally ill will eventually lead to involuntary euthanasia is called the "slippery slope" argument. Not all Americans find it convincing.

Proponents of legalization say that safeguards against abuse can work. They point to Oregon's experience with legalized assisted suicide as a perfect example of how the practice can be contained. According to the Death with Dignity National Center, by carefully defining who would be eligible for physician-assisted suicide, Oregon lawmakers made the Death with Dignity Act virtually foolproof. The organization points to the following requirements as proof of the law's adequate safeguards:

- The patient must make two oral requests to his or her physician, separated by at least fifteen days.

- The patient must provide a written request to his or her physician witnessed by two individuals who are not family members or primary caregivers.

- A patient may rescind his or her request at any time.

- The diagnosis and prognosis must be confirmed by the prescribing physician and a consulting physician.

- The prescribing physician and a consulting physician must concur that the patient is capable (defined as able to make and communicate health care decisions).

- If either physician determines that the patient's judgment is impaired, the patient must be referred for a psychological examination.

- The prescribing physician must inform the patient of alternatives, including palliative care, hospice, and pain management options.

With data accumulating on how Oregon's Death with Dignity Act is working, those engaged in the debate over euthanasia will have more insight into whether the slippery slope argument is in fact convincing. The viewpoints in this chapter examine other issues concerning legalized euthanasia's effect on society.

"If death is a 'benefit' for competent patients suffering from a certain condition, why should it be denied incompetent patients suffering from the same condition?"

Legalizing Voluntary Euthanasia Would Lead to Nonvoluntary Euthanasia

John Shelby Keown

John Shelby Keown, the author of Euthanasia Examined *and* Euthanasia, Ethics, and Public Policy: An Argument Against Legalisation, *from which this viewpoint is excerpted, argues that legalizing voluntary euthanasia would inevitably lead to involuntary euthanasia. He contends that no regulatory scheme would be sufficient to confine the practice to only those cases where the patient makes a well-informed decision to die. Another problem with legalization, according to Keown, is that if doctors agree that death would benefit some patients who ask for it, nothing will stop them from thinking that other patients who do not ask to die are also better off dead.*

As you read, consider the following questions:

1. What does Keown say is a misapplication of the empirical argument?

2. How might doctors fail in regard to voluntary euthanasia, in the author's opinion?

3. What "catch 22" does Keown outline in regard to legalization of VAE?

The prohibition of VAE [Voluntary Active Euthanasia] by the criminal laws of almost all countries and by the ethical codes of virtually all medical associations testifies to the historic and enduring appeal of the principle of the inviolability of human life. Many people continue to judge that it is wrong intentionally to take the life of another person, even if that person earnestly requests death to avoid pain and suffering. Many, therefore, continue to oppose VAE in principle.

But many do not. They believe that in principle, VAE (or at least PAS [Physician-Assisted Suicide]) is morally justifiable provided that the patient's request is free and informed, and that the patient is suffering from an illness resulting in unbearable suffering which can only be ended by terminating the patient's life. However, it does not follow that they also believe that the law should therefore be relaxed to permit VAE or PAS. Many such people oppose relaxation of the law because they believe it would result in (or would involve an unacceptable risk of resulting in) two undesirable consequences. The first is a slide from PAS to VAE and from VAE to NVAE [Non-Voluntary Active Euthanasia] and possibly even IVAE [Involuntary Active Euthanasia]. The second is a slide from VAE as a last resort to its use as a standard and premature alternative to palliative care. In short, many of those who see nothing wrong with VAE *in principle* do not want the law to permit it *in practice* because they think it would be likely to result in a slide down a slippery slope from something they condone—ending patients' lives at their request as a last resort—to something they oppose—ending their lives without request or where less extreme alternatives exist. The slippery slope argument about what is likely to happen in practice has taken centre-stage in the contemporary debate. It therefore merits close consideration.

The Nature of the Slippery Slope Argument

The slippery slope argument holds that if a proposal is made to accept A, which is not agreed to be morally objectionable, it should nevertheless be rejected because it would lead to B, which is agreed to be morally objectionable. An illustration would be the argument that it is wrong to permit abortion, even on health grounds, because even if abortion on health grounds were morally acceptable, allowing it will tend to lead to abortion for social convenience, which is not. . . .

Sometimes the empirical argument can be misapplied. It would clearly be pressing the argument too far to argue that no one should touch a drop of alcohol because of the risk of alcoholism. The vast majority of people are able to make common-sense judgments about how much they can safely drink without becoming addicted. Nor is the taking of alcohol as such morally contested issue (at least in secular society). Abortion is, however, a hotly disputed moral issue, and the difficulty of justifying, drawing and policing a distinction between 'medical' and 'social' grounds for abortion gives the slippery slope argument against allowing abortion for 'medical' reasons much greater purchase. In short, the slippery slope argument sometimes has force, and sometimes lacks force. The question here is whether it has force in relation to the legalisation of VAE.

The slippery slope argument is often thought of as one argument but it is more accurately understood as comprising two independent arguments: the 'logical' and the 'empirical'.

The Practical Slippery Slope Argument

The empirical slippery slope argument runs that even if a line can in principle be drawn between VAE and NVAE, and between VAE as a last resort and as an earlier resort, a slide will occur in practice because the safeguards to prevent it cannot be made effective. In other words, purely as a *practical* matter, VAE resists effective regulation. Try as one may to devise procedures to ensure that it is only performed after a clear and considered request by the patient, and only where it is a last resort, there will in practice be an inevitable tendency for it to be performed in cases where the request is neither clear nor considered, and where alternatives are available but are overlooked or even deliberately ignored. And the reason that the empirical argument has force in relation to VAE, it may be claimed, is that it is no more possible to frame precise guidelines for VAE, and to police doctors' interpretation and application of those guidelines, than it is possible to frame and police guidelines for 'therapeutic' abortion.

Any attempt at effective legal regulation of VAE will break down, the argument runs, because some—perhaps many—doctors will fail to ensure that requests are genuine, free and considered, and that there are no alternatives. Some doctors will fail because, although they are conscientious practitioners with the best interests of their patients at heart, they simply lack the psychiatric expertise to discern when a request is the result not of the patient's free and considered judgment but of clinical depression. Others will fail because, although they may have, or have theoretical access to, the required expertise, they lack the time or resources to apply or access it in practice. Still others will fail because they are not sufficiently conscientious to consider the quality of the patient's request.

Equally, some doctors will fail to ensure that VAE is used only as a last resort. In some cases, patients will be misdiagnosed and inaccurately told their condition is terminal. Other patients will be correctly diagnosed but will be given a false prognosis: the doctor will mistakenly tell the patient there is no hope of a cure. And in some cases, even when the doctor arrives at a correct diagnosis and prognosis, he will simply

Doctors Will Grow More Comfortable with Killing

If we are asking assistance in ... suicide, there is at least one medical doctor involved. If assisted suicide becomes legal, some doctors will no doubt assert their continuing commitment to the Hippocratic oath and refuse to participate in it. But many doctors will adjust their practices, and gradually their values, as well. Initially, some will simply desire to help patients in this final act, and some will feel it part of their medical responsibility to do so, regardless of their personal desires. Insofar as assisted suicide is a cost-efficient means of death, doctors are also likely to be rewarded by healthcare companies for participating in it. As institutional expectations and rewards increasingly favor assisted suicide, expectations and rewards within the medical profession itself will gradually shift to reflect this. Medical students will learn about assisted suicide as an important patient option from the beginning of their training. We may expect that a growing proportion of doctors will find themselves sympathetic to this practice, and will find themselves comfortable with recommending it to their patients.

Patricia S. Mann, "Meanings of Death,"
Physician-Assisted Suicide: Expanding
the Debate, 1998.

lack sufficient expertise in palliative care to know what relief it can offer the particular patient.

Again, the parallel with abortion may assist. How many doctors have the expertise, commitment, time and resources to consider the quality of each request for abortion in appropriate depth? Surely some, perhaps many if not most, approve requests for abortion after a relatively brief consultation and without any expert psychiatric evaluation of the woman. How many requests for abortion have been granted which were really the result of clinical depression or pressure from spouses, partners or relatives? And how many women experience lasting psychological harm and psychiatric illness as a result of abortions which were really someone *else's* choice? In VAE, of course, the quality of the decision is no less crucial and merits no less attention given the particular vulnerability to pressure of the elderly dying and the significant proportion of patients requesting VAE who are in fact clinically depressed.

Again, in how many cases is abortion used truly as a last resort? In how many cases are women presented with realistic alternatives, whether it be in the form of help from social services, or specialist advice about bringing up a disabled child? If VAE were to follow in the footsteps of abortion, would it not frequently be performed with inadequate examination of the quality of the request and little if any exploration of alternatives? And given that in the VAE debate, unlike the abortion debate, there is no dispute that the life at stake is that of a full human being, the argument for caution is recognisably clearer. The analogy between abortion and VAE is not exact, but if anything the differences (the particular vulnerability of the debilitated and dying elderly, who would, at least initially, tend to be the prime candidates) serve only to sharpen the slippery slope argument against VAE. . . .

Could Guidelines Stop the Slide?

Could it not be argued, however, that appropriately strict guidelines would forestall any slide down the empirical slope? Guidelines which would ensure that each request was properly checked, that the diagnosis and prognosis were confirmed, that alternatives were fully investigated, and that the patient's suffering was truly unbearable? The empirical argument questions the possibility of drafting and enforcing such safeguards. How, for example, does a guideline purport to ensure that a request is truly 'voluntary'? How can a doctor know whether the request reflects the true, considered and informed wishes of the patient, or is a result of pressure from relatives? And how can a guideline ensure that the patient's suffering is truly 'unbearable'?

Surely, guidelines would end up granting considerable leeway to the opinion of the doctor as to whether the request was voluntary, and to the feelings of the patient as to whether the suffering was unbearable. Both of these are recalcitrant to external regulation. Moreover, even if precise guidelines could be formulated, specifying what qualifies as a 'voluntary' request and 'unbearable' suffering, how could the guidelines be effectively enforced?

Here advocates of VAE appear to encounter yet another 'catch-22'. One approach to regulation is to avoid independent scrutiny of the doctor's actions and to trust to the doctor's competence and good faith. But then how is either incompetence or dishonesty to be prevented? A stricter approach is to build in stringent independent checks, such as the prior, or at least retrospective, approval of an independent person or body, such as a lawyer or a court. But how many doctors are likely to submit themselves and their patients to an independent review, particularly by a lawyer? Any middle approach, such as requiring consultation with an independent doctor, might well prove to be more form than substance. Though a doctor would be less reluctant to consult another doctor than a judge, how likely is the second doctor to conduct an independent examination of the patient, familiarise himself with all the facts of the case, and rigorously scrutinise the competence and good faith of the first doctor? The tendency of some second-opinion doctors to 'rubber-stamp' the opinion of the first is certainly far from unknown in other contexts. . . . Moreover, the tendency of doctors to overlook their colleagues' unprofessional behaviour is well documented.

After a comprehensive review of proposals to decriminalise PAS in the USA, philosopher Daniel Callahan and lawyer

Margot White concluded that *none* of the proposals would have ensured effective regulation. They observed: 'The fundamental problem with legalization of PAS and euthanasia lies in the nature of the physician-patient relationship—that it is conducted in private and protected by ethical and legal requirements of confidentiality. Therefore, it is inherently inconsistent with on-site procedural requirements.'

They added that legalisation could serve only to protect the physician, not the patient: 'It will not, and cannot, achieve the goal of protecting patients or of preventing or limiting abuse. If protection of patients and meaningful regulation of PAS/euthanasia is the goal, no legislation can achieve it.'

Years ago, in his classic article refuting the case for the legalisation or VAE, Professor Yale Kamisar, the distinguished liberal scholar of US constitutional law, noted that campaigners for VAE were seeking a goal which is inherently inconsistent: a procedure for death which provides ample safeguards against abuse and mistake, and one which is 'quick' and 'easy' in operation.

In short, the empirical argument maintains that guidelines, whether lax or strict, cannot guarantee effective regulation of the doctor's decision-making. Indeed, stricter guidelines may serve to make doctors even *less* compliant. Hence, the regulatory 'catch-22' which appears to beset any attempt to permit VAE subject to 'guidelines' or 'safeguards': any attempt to close the hand of regulation more tightly may well result in more cases slipping, unregulated, through its fingers. Even leaving aside the grave difficulty if not practical impossibility of policing VAE, there remains another reason why, it is argued, a slide will occur. . . .

The Logical Slippery Slope Argument

[The logical argument] holds that, even if precise guidelines could be framed which sought to permit only VAE in cases of unbearable suffering, those guidelines would soon give way, not (or not only) because of practical difficulties of enforcement *but because the case for euthanasia with those limitations is also, logically, a case for euthanasia without them.*

The logical argument runs that acceptance of VAE leads to acceptance of NVAE because the former rests on the judgment that some patients would be better off dead, which judgment can logically be made even if the patient is incapable of making a request. The proposals currently advanced by advocates of VAE and PAS envisage a central role for doctors, not only in the termination of life itself, but also in the decision to terminate life. They are not proposals for 'euthanasia on demand', that is, simply at the patient's request and without the considered assessment, judgment and approval of a responsible doctor.

Doctors are not robots who mindlessly comply with their patients' wishes. They are professionals who form their own judgment about the merits of any request for medical intervention. A responsible doctor would not agree to kill a patient just because the patient autonomously asked, any more than the doctor would prescribe anti-depressant drugs for a patient just because the patient autonomously requested them. The doctor, if acting professionally, would decide in each case whether the intervention was truly in the patient's best interests. Therefore, a responsible doctor would no more kill a patient who had, in the doctor's opinion, 'a life worth living' than prescribe anti-depressants for a patient who, in the doctor's opinion, was not depressed. Advocates of VAE would surely agree. They typically propose VAE only for those who meet certain conditions, whether 'terminal illness' or 'unbearable suffering', which it is thought makes their lives no longer worth living.

Consequently, the real, rather than the rhetorical, justification for VAE is not the patient's autonomous request *but the doctor's judgment that the request is justified because death would benefit the patient.* True, in the proposals currently advanced by campaigners for VAE, this judgment would not be made without a prior, autonomous request by the patient. But even under such proposals the autonomous request is not decisive. It serves merely to trigger the *doctor's* judgment about the merits of the request. To put the point more crudely, the patient proposes but the *doctor* disposes. The *doctor* decides whether the request is justified, that is, whether the patient would indeed be better off dead. And if a doctor can make this judgment in relation to an autonomous patient, a doctor can, logically, make it in relation to an incompetent patient. Moreover, if death is a 'benefit' for competent patients suffering from a certain condition, why should it be denied incompetent patients suffering from the same condition?

Going from Competent to Incompetent Patient

If VAE were to be made available to competent people who requested it, it would soon be argued that it should be extended to the incompetent, either on the ground that it would be discriminatory to deny them this benefit because of their incompetence or because VAE is what they would have wanted had they been competent to ask for it. The latter approach, which constructs what is called a 'substituted judgment' on behalf of the incompetent, is already well established in the law relating to the treatment of incompetent patients in parts of the USA. . . .

VAE supporters may well disagree, and press the argument that it is ultimately the *patient* who decides whether his life is worth while, but this argument sits uneasily with their own typical legislative proposals which require a *doctor,* exercising independent judgment, to approve the patient's request. The doctor's role is not envisaged simply as one of ensuring that the patient's request is autonomous (indeed, a psychologist or counsellor would surely discharge that function at least as well), but as one of considering the *merits* of the request.

What could those merits be other than a judgment that the patient would indeed be better off dead? And once doctors began to make comprehensive judgments of that sort in relation to competent people, why would they not think themselves equally qualified to make such judgments in relation to incompetent patients? Why should they deny their incompetent patients the benefit of euthanasia when they are in exactly the same situation as their competent patients, except for their ability to request that benefit? Is there any other situation in medical practice where doctors deny treatment which they think beneficial simply because the patient cannot request it?. . .

Unbearable Suffering Is Not a Logical Criterion

Those advocates of VAE who insist that what is decisive in justifying VAE is respect for individual autonomy encounter a logical problem if they also insist that VAE be limited to patients who are suffering unbearably. For if VAE is justified by respect for patient self-determination, how can it be right to deny it to any patient who autonomously asks for it, whether or not they are experiencing 'unbearable suffering'? Why need their suffering be 'unbearable'?. . . What if a patient earnestly asks for VAE because, say, he is suffering from some incurable condition such as severe arthritis, which is which is painful and debilitating and which, even though it may be bearable, he does not want to bear? The case would be even stronger if he had previously led a life in which physical activity, such as outdoor pursuits, had played a central part. Indeed, the patient may have a condition which involves relatively little physical suffering. Imagine a rock-climbing fanatic who has been paralysed from the neck down in a climbing accident and who requests VAE because he says that he 'does not want to live trapped in a useless body'. Why should he be denied release if he believes that life has lost its value?. . .

If the core justification for VAE is thought to be respect for patient autonomy, this is surely logically inconsistent with a requirement that the patient be suffering unbearably, bearably, or at all. . . .

'Hard cases', say lawyers, 'make bad law.' However tempting it may be to make exceptions in difficult cases, the effect of so doing may be that the exception swallows the rule. The temptation to pull shipwreck survivors into a full lifeboat may be strong, but it should be resisted lest the lifeboat capsize. Both of the slippery slope arguments urge that, however tempting it may be for the law to accommodate 'mercy killing' in extreme circumstances, yielding to the temptation would subvert the law's protection of all. . . . The argument has persuaded many that legalisation would be a mistake—even many of those who support VAE in principle.

"So long as we retain a firm criterion of free and informed consent, the logical slide to involuntary assisted death will not be a problem."

Legalizing Voluntary Euthanasia Would Not Lead to Nonvoluntary Euthanasia

Jocelyn Downie

In the following viewpoint Jocelyn Downie contends that legalizing assisted suicide will not automatically lead to involuntary euthanasia. According to Downie, as long as laws are written that clearly define the criteria of who can be assisted to die, people outside that defined group will be safe from non-voluntary euthanasia. Moreover, although Downie concedes that there have been cases of abuse in The Netherlands, where physician-assisted suicide is legal, she claims that euthanasia in that country is not widespread, and people have not accepted the practice of nonvoluntary euthanasia. The Dutch example shows that legalizing assisted suicide need not result in the widespread killing of patients without their consent. Downie is the director of the Health Law Institute and an associate professor of law and medicine at Dalhousie Law School in Nova Scotia, Canada.

As you read, consider the following questions:

Jocelyn Downie, *Dying Justice: A Case for Decriminalizing Euthanasia in Canada.* Toronto: University of Toronto Press, 2004. Copyright © 2004 by the University of Toronto Press, Inc. Reproduced by permission.

1. What slippery slope example besides euthanasia does Downie give using the Nazi experience?
2. What two cautions does the author give about the incidence of euthanasia in The Netherlands?
3. How does Downie suggest avoiding the slippery slopes for euthanasia and for the withdrawal or withholding of treatment?

The slippery slope argument is commonly expressed in the following terms. If society allows assisted suicide and voluntary euthanasia, then there will be a slide towards the bottom of a slippery slope and many clearly unacceptable practices will become prevalent. For example, it is feared that we will soon find ourselves unable to prevent involuntary euthanasia of the elderly, the disabled, and other vulnerable individuals. Once it is accepted that one particular life is not worth living and can be deliberately terminated, then there will be no good (or persuasive) reason to claim that the lives of the disabled, the elderly, and other vulnerable people are worth living. To prevent such an undesirable result, all lives must be valued and assisted suicide and voluntary euthanasia must not be permitted.

There are two forms of slippery slopes: logical; and empirical. In the interest of analytical clarity, I examine each type independently.

The Logical Slippery Slope

The logical slippery slope argument takes the following form: if we allow assisted suicide and voluntary euthanasia, we will not be able to draw any logical distinction between acceptable and unacceptable killings, and, hence, we will slide towards the bottom of the slope (i.e., towards allowing involuntary euthanasia and thus the killing of demented, mentally handicapped, and indigent persons as well as any other group deemed 'unfit' for continued existence).

However, if a logically sustainable distinction can be drawn between the evaluation of life at the top of the slope and the evaluation of life at the bottom of the slope, then we have sufficient materials to erect a barrier on the slope. In other words, if reasons for allowing the activities at the top do not logically entail reasons for allowing activities at the bottom, then the descent is not logically necessary. Since we can distinguish between different evaluations (e.g., evaluations of the value of life made by the subject and evaluations of the value of life made by another person), we can avoid the logical slippery slope even if we allow assisted suicide and voluntary euthanasia. So long as we retain a firm criterion of free and informed consent, the logical slide to involuntary assisted death will not be a problem.

The Empirical Slippery Slope

The empirical slippery slope argument is not so easily addressed. The argument here is that once certain practices are accepted, people shall in fact go on to accept other practices as well. This is simply a claim about what people will do, and not a claim about what they are logically committed to, [in the words of James Rachels]. Clearly, this version of the slippery slope argument is more difficult for advocates of assisted suicide and voluntary euthanasia.

Obviously, we have no direct empirical data on whether people . . . would in fact over the next five, ten, or twenty years move from accepting assisted suicide and voluntary euthanasia to accepting involuntary euthanasia. Indeed, it is doubtful that any study could be designed to gather that data without tracking practice in a trial period of regulated but decriminalized assisted suicide and voluntary euthanasia. In the absence of such specific data, many turn to history and to other countries in search of evidence as to whether slippage would in fact follow decriminalization. This is where a careful analysis of the historical experience of the Nazis and the contemporary experience of the Netherlands becomes relevant.

The notorious death camps of Nazi Germany are frequently offered as evidence of human inability to avoid descent down the empirical slippery slope. Indeed, there is no denying that the Nazi regime established a horrific program of murder and genocide under the banner euthanasia. However, caution must be exercised in drawing conclusions from the Nazi experience about what people . . . in the beginning of the twenty-first century will in fact do if assisted suicide and voluntary euthanasia are decriminalized. There are a number of significant differences between the Nazi experience and the contemporary Canadian movement to decriminalize assisted suicide and voluntary euthanasia.

First, the Nazi program did not slide from voluntary to involuntary. It was, from the beginning, involuntary. . . . Second, the Nazi program was motivated by jingoism, racism, and a fascist political ideology. By contrast, the movement to decriminalize assisted suicide and voluntary euthanasia is motivated by a desire to alleviate suffering and respect individual autonomy. Third, pre-Nazi Germany did not have as a part of its collective consciousness an awareness of the horrors of the Holocaust. The example of Nazi Germany could actually deter the very slippage it is taken to indicate is possible.

Nazi Euthanasia Compared to Human Experimentation

In addition, one can apply the technique of *retorqueo argumentum* (turning the argument back on the one who uses it) on the Nazi analogy. For if the Nazi practice of involuntary euthanasia precludes voluntary euthanasia, then the Nazi practice of involuntary research involving humans precludes voluntary research involving humans. Absent from discussions of euthanasia relying on the Nazi analogy is a recognition of the

Slippery Slope Arguments Are Invalid

[One] argument against voluntary active euthanasia is the Slippery Slope argument—if we allow active euthanasia, it will lead to terrible abuses. . . .

The Slippery Slope argument is weak. . . . The fact that a practice *can be abused* does not mean that it shouldn't be used at all. Salt and sugar can be abused and harm us, but that doesn't mean that they shouldn't be used at all—even for legitimate purposes. Knives, cars, and drugs can be abused, but that doesn't mean that they should be outlawed.

We can well imagine serious abuses of the right to die. Imagine Aunt Ann, dying of cancer. She is running up large hospital and doctor bills, depleting her savings. Now Nephew Ned, who figures to collect handsomely from Aunt Ann's estate, is certain that Aunt Ann would be better off dead than alive. He encourages Aunt Ann to come to the same conclusion before her estate becomes bankrupt. We would want to take measures to prevent such manipulation, but if we became convinced that we could not control them, we might well concede that voluntary active euthanasia, while in principle moral, should not become legal.

Difficult as it may be, we can safeguard terminally ill patients from most manipulative practices, so the slippery slope argument isn't obviously valid here. The lesson of the argument is to put in place measures that will protect patients from abuse, while still respecting patient autonomy.

> Louis P. Pojman, *Life and Death: Grappling with the Moral Dilemmas of Our Time*, 2000.

fact that the Nazi regime conducted horrific experiments on non-consenting humans. . . .

The Nazi experience with research involving humans is rightly advanced as a chilling reminder of the need to be vigilant with respect to the regulation of research involving humans, but it is not advanced as grounds to prohibit voluntary human experimentation. Unless one is willing to accept a prohibition on all research involving humans, one cannot consistently use the Nazi experience with involuntary euthanasia as grounds to prohibit assisted suicide or voluntary euthanasia.

One response to this *retorqueo* might be to say that we are simply as a matter of fact less likely to slide from voluntary experimentation to involuntary experimentation than we are to slide from voluntary euthanasia to involuntary euthanasia. Therefore, the Nazi experience with involuntary experimentation need serve only as a caveat but the Nazi experience with involuntary euthanasia can serve as an absolute block. However, there is evidence that we are capable of sliding from voluntary experimentation to involuntary experimentation. The experiences of the Tuskegee Syphilis study and the Allan Memorial Hospital 'brainwashing' studies, for example, vividly illustrate our capacity to slide down the Nazi slope.

This *retorqueo argumentum* does not disprove the claim that the Nazi experience is evidence of the empirical slippery slope. However, the argument does raise serious questions about the application and force of the proposed analogy between the Nazi experience and decriminalization of assisted suicide and euthanasia. . . .

The Netherlands Has Not Gone Down the Slope

Another analogy is frequently drawn to current practice in the Netherlands. Some argue the Netherlands moved to a permissive regime regarding assisted suicide and voluntary euthanasia and then slid down the slope to involuntary euthanasia. [Herbert] Hendlin et al. claim that during the past 2 decades, the Netherlands has moved from considering assisted suicide (preferred over euthanasia by the Dutch Voluntary Euthanasia Society) to giving legal sanction to both physician-assisted suicide and euthanasia, from euthanasia for terminally ill patients to euthanasia for those who are chronically ill, from euthanasia for physical illness to euthanasia for psychological distress, and from voluntary euthanasia to non-voluntary and involuntary euthanasia. . . .

The implication is that [other countries], too, would slide to the objectionable bottom of the empirical slippery slope if we decriminalize assisted suicide and voluntary euthanasia.

While the Dutch experience should give us some concern about an empirical slippery slope, it should not give us the level of concern suggested by these commentators. . . . The Dutch experience does not provide a basis on which to conclude that assisted suicide and voluntary euthanasia should not be decriminalized [elsewhere].

It should be emphasized here that I am not claiming that the Dutch experience provides a positive basis for decriminalizing assisted suicide and euthanasia. . . .

Rather, I am making a negative rather than a positive claim. . . . I am denying . . . that the Netherlands has slid down the slippery slope. My discussion of the Netherlands experience has the narrow purpose of assessing the validity of the use of the Netherlands existence with assisted death as evidence of the force of the slippery slope argument against decriminalization.

Much has been written about the Dutch experience with respect to assisted death. Unfortunately, a lot of what has been written has either misinterpreted or misrepresented the Dutch situation, and this has greatly clouded the debate about the significance of the Dutch experience for . . . public policy. . . .

Euthanasia Is Not Widespread

Some proponents of the empirical slippery slope argument claim that euthanasia is widespread in the Netherlands. Richard Fenigsen, for example, claims: The findings published in the report indicate that annually 25,306 cases of euthanasia (as defined by Fletcher) occur in the Netherlands . . . The 25,306 cases of euthanasia constitute 19.4% of the 130,000 deaths that occur in the Netherlands each year. Hendlin et al. claim: 'Given legal sanction, euthanasia, intended originally for the exceptional case, has become an accepted way of dealing with serious or terminal illness in the Netherlands.'

Such claims about the incidence of euthanasia in the Netherlands demand two cautions. First, a great deal of confusion and equivocation surrounds the term 'euthanasia.' The authors of the report referred to by Fenigsen include only voluntary active euthanasia in the term 'euthanasia,' while Fenigsen and many other opponents of a permissive regime with respect to assisted death include the withholding and withdrawal of potentially life-sustaining treatment and the provision of potentially life-shortening palliative treatment in the term. Thus, on the basis of the same data, one group concludes that there are 2,300 cases per year of euthanasia and the other concludes that there are 25,306. On the latter definition, euthanasia is obviously far more widespread than on the former. However, on the latter, euthanasia is also far less morally problematic and controversial than on the former.

Second, the claim that euthanasia (defined narrowly) is widespread is simply not supported by the data. Two major studies have been commissioned by the Dutch government; one in 1990 and one in 1995. In 1990, 1.8 per cent of deaths resulted from euthanasia and 0.3 per cent resulted from assisted suicide. In 1995, 2.4 per cent resulted from euthanasia and 0.3 per cent resulted from assisted suicide.

Euthanasia Is Not Available on Demand

The claim that euthanasia is available on demand can mean, first, that all requests for euthanasia are granted and, second, that euthanasia will be performed almost immediately upon request. Neither claim is true. Consider each in turn.

The 1995 study mentioned above revealed that there are approximately 10,000 concrete requests for euthanasia and assisted suicide each year and that approximately 6,000 are not carried out (because the physician refuses in approximately 3,000 cases and the patient dies before the request can be honoured in most of the other cases). Thus, only about one-third of requests for euthanasia or assisted suicide actually result in a death by euthanasia or assisted suicide. . . .

Non-Voluntary Euthanasia Is Not Widespread

Prior to the publication of the Remmelink Report, claims were made that non-voluntary euthanasia was widespread in the Netherlands. For example, Fenigsen stated that '[t]here is now ample evidence that 'voluntary' euthanasia is accompanied by the practice of crypthanasia (active euthanasia on sick people without their knowledge).'

Following the publication of the report, these claims were reiterated with what was taken to be proof found in the report; the report is frequently cited as revealing that there are 1,000 cases of non-voluntary euthanasia every year in the Netherlands.

At least two responses can be made to this charge. First, care must be taken with the definition of the term 'non-voluntary euthanasia' (or Fenigsen's 'crypthanasia'). In assessing the truth and moral weight of an empirical claim about the incidence of non-voluntary euthanasia, the reader must be sure whether or not the claimant includes within euthanasia the withholding and withdrawal of potentially life-sustaining treatment and the provision of potentially life-shortening palliative treatment.

Second, an analysis of the data shows that non-voluntary euthanasia (as defined by the Remmelink Report, the Senate Committee on Euthanasia and Assisted Suicide, and this book, e.g., lethal injection of potassium chloride where the wishes of the individual are not known) is not widespread. The oft-cited 1,000 figure comes from a study that concluded that 0.8-percent of deaths resulted from LAWER (life-terminating acts without explicit request of patient). . . .

In 600 of the 1,000 cases, something about the patient's wishes was known although explicit consent according to the legal guidelines had not been given. In only 400 cases were the wishes not known at all. Quite clearly, the data on the incidence of LAWER in the Netherlands do not support a claim of widespread non-voluntary euthanasia. They do support a claim of some non-voluntary euthanasia but arguably considerably less than the projected 1,000 cases per year.

Richard Fenigsen has claimed that 'crypthanasia is not an "abuse" of the practice of voluntary euthanasia; it is widely accepted, openly supported, and praised as a charitable deed.' John Keown has reported 'growing condonation' and 'growing support' for non-voluntary euthanasia in the Netherlands. However, no empirical data support the claim that non-voluntary euthanasia is increasingly accepted. The incidence did not increase between 1990 and 1995. If incidence reflects acceptance, then there is no evidence of increasing acceptance. More significantly, the incidence of non-voluntary euthanasia uncovered by the 1990 study was a source of both concern and action on the part of the Dutch authorities as well as many proponents of the Dutch regime. . . .

Preventing the Slippery Slope

It should first be noted that there is good reason to be concerned about the situation in the Netherlands. As we have already seen, non-voluntary euthanasia and non-voluntary withholding and withdrawal of potentially life-sustaining treatment are all occurring. Procedural guidelines are not always followed. For example, appropriate consultation and reporting do not always occur. The safeguards intended to protect the vulnerable do not appear, at least as currently implemented, to be sufficient. However, no conclusions follow about decriminalizing assisted suicide and euthanasia [elsewhere]. At least the following responses to the Netherlands-based slippery slope argument can be made.

A critical step in the slippery slope argument is that increased permissiveness caused the slide down the slippery slope; if that is not true, then the Netherlands-based empirical slippery slope argument against decriminalization loses its force. However, there is no evidence that the shift in policy and practice with respect to the state's response to euthanasia and assisted suicide in the Netherlands caused any slide down a slippery slope. . . .

Non-voluntary Euthanasia Happens Elsewhere

The slippery slope argument is also grounded in the assumption that the incidence of non-voluntary euthanasia is higher in the Netherlands than in those countries where it is illegal without grounds for immunity from prosecution. The truth of this assumption has not been empirically demonstrated and indeed there are now data to suggest that the assumption is false. [Helga Kuhse and other] authors of a recent [1997] Australian study summarized their results as follows: "The proportion of all Australian deaths that involved a medical end-of-life decision were: euthanasia, 1.8% (including physician-assisted suicide, 0.1%); ending of patient's life without patient's concurrent explicit request, 3.5%; withholding or withdrawing of potentially life-prolonging treatment, 28.6%; alleviation of pain with opioids in doses large enough that there was a probable life-shortening effect, 30.9%. In 30% of all Australian deaths, a medical end-of-life decision was made with the explicit intention of ending the patient's life, of which 4% were in response to a direct request from the patient. Overall, Australia had a higher rate of intentional ending of life without the patient's request than the Netherlands."

The authors concluded that 'Australian law has not prevented doctors from practising euthanasia or making medical end-of-life decisions explicitly intended to hasten the patient's death without the patient's request.' [John] Griffiths et al. also provide the following as support for their dismissal of the comparative international slippery slope argument: Recent research in the United States gives rates of assistance with suicide roughly comparable to the Dutch figure for euthanasia. . . . These facts cast even more doubt on the use of the Netherlands in the empirical slippery slope argument against decriminalization of assisted death.

Finally, it should also be noted, from a comparative international perspective, that there is evidence of societies decriminalizing assisted suicide and/or voluntary euthanasia and not sliding down the slippery slope to involuntary euthanasia. Indeed, examples point in the opposite direction. Infanticide has been practised in numerous cultures around the world without any of these cultures sliding to involuntary euthanasia. Senicide was practised by Inuit cultures again without any slide to involuntary euthanasia. Assisted suicide has not been illegal in Switzerland for many years without a slide. Oregon decriminalized assisted suicide in 1997 and has not witnessed any precipitous slide down the slippery slope. The comparative international empirical data are thus, for the proponents of the slippery slope argument, at best mixed and, at worst, counter to their argument. . . .

If slippage from voluntary euthanasia to non-voluntary or involuntary euthanasia is possible, then slippage is also possible down the slope from voluntary to non-voluntary and involuntary withholding and withdrawal of potentially life-sustaining treatment. So long as the danger of the slippery slope does not preclude these latter sorts of assisted death practices, it cannot preclude assisted suicide and voluntary euthanasia.

The empirical slippery slope is a matter for serious concern. However, the solution to the concern must be the same for assisted suicide and voluntary euthanasia as for the withholding and withdrawal of potentially life-sustaining treatment. The solution is not to prohibit any particular form(s) of assisted death but rather to be vigilant with respect to the satisfaction of the necessary conditions for permissible assisted death.

> *"Since legalizing assisted suicide, Oregonians have seen first-hand what really happens . . . safeguards don't work."*

Oregon's Assisted Suicide Experience: Safeguards Do Not Work

Oregon Right to Life

Oregon Right to Life (ORTL) argues in the following viewpoint that legal assisted suicide is dangerous because safeguards built into the law do not work. ORTL points to numerous cases in Oregon—where physician-assisted suicide is legal—to show how legalization leads to abuses. Depressed or demented patients have been euthanized, the authors contend, rather than receive treatment for their mental conditions, for example. Oregon Right to Life, based in Salem, Oregon, is opposed to abortion, infanticide, and euthanasia.

As you read, consider the following questions:

1. What does the organization cite as the main concern about physician-assisted suicide?
2. In ORTL's view, what problem does the Matheny case reveal?
3. What percentage of patients who used the assisted suicide law received psychiatric counseling by the seventh year?

Oregon Right to Life, "Oregon's Assisted Suicide Experience: Safeguards Don't Work," www.ortl.org, 2005. Reproduced by permission.

On November 8, 1994, Oregon became the first government in the world to legalize physician-assisted suicide. The law was ruled unconstitutional due to unequal protection under the law. "What are the boundary lines, if any, to state-sanctioned suicide?" the federal judge asked (*Lee v. Oregon*). "Where in the Constitution do we find distinctions between the terminally ill with six months to live, the terminally ill with one year to live, paraplegics, the disabled, or any category of people who have their own reasons for not wanting to continue living?" In 1997 the Ninth Circuit Court overturned the decision on the grounds that the plaintiffs did not have legal standing to bring the case to court. In November of 1997 a measure which would have repealed the law was rejected by Oregon voters. Oregon became the first jurisdiction in the world to begin experimenting with legalized assisted suicide.

Defining Physician-Assisted Suicide

It is important to distinguish between physician-assisted suicide and refusing medical treatment. Physician-assisted suicide involves a physician prescribing lethal drugs for a patient with the knowledge that the patient intends to use the drugs to commit suicide. Refusing medical treatment is turning down treatment expected to prolong life. What does this mean? Refusing a ventilator, or some other life sustaining machine or treatment is not assisted suicide and is already legal in all states. The intent of refusing medical treatment is not to end life, but to allow nature to take its course. With physician-assisted suicide the intent is to kill the patient. Euthanasia is the lethal injection of the patient by the doctor.

In the 1997 Supreme Court case, *Washington v. Glucksberg*, physician-assisted suicide was rejected as a constitutional right because "the right to autonomy clashes with the right to life in our constitutional system. . . . Death is the extinguishment of rights, not the triumph of one right over another." The U.S. Supreme Court upheld both the New York and Washington

Abuses Also Occur in the Netherlands

When we read that 900 patients were deliberately killed without their request in 1995 (a figure which rose to 980 in 2001) we should remember that this figure, alarming as it is, does not include 1,537 cases where palliative drugs were given with the explicit, unrequested aim of hastening death. If we include this group of cases, it becomes clear that more than a third of those actively killed were killed non-voluntarily.

The Linacre Center for Healthcare Ethics,
"Submission to the House of Lords Select Committee
on the Assisted Dying for the Terminally Ill Bill," September 2004.

statutes prohibiting assisted suicide in all cases by a 9-0 vote. Physician-assisted suicide is not a right protected by our Constitution.

Legalization Is Dangerous

Opponents of assisted suicide are concerned about the many abuses that could occur if it is legalized. In addition to the many dangerous effects that opponents and judges feel it would have on society's attitudes towards suicide, they are concerned about:

- The power and pressures placed on physicians and how it will affect their role as healer.

- Protecting vulnerable groups including the poor, the elderly, and disabled persons from abuse, neglect and mistakes: "No matter how carefully any guidelines are framed, assisted suicide and euthanasia will be practiced through the prism of social inequality and bias that characterizes the delivery of services in all segments of all society, including health care," [wrote the New York Task Force].

- Health care cost containment: "The growing concern about health care cost increases the risks presented by legalizing assisted suicide and euthanasia," [according to the New York Task Force].

The main concern about physician-assisted suicide is the inability to create safeguards or contain assisted suicide to any boundaries. In ruling Oregon's law unconstitutional the federal judge stated that if assisted suicide is legalized, it must be legal for everyone: "The attempt to restrict such rights to the terminally ill is illusory" (*Lee v. Oregon*).

Advocates of physician-assisted suicide claim that it is meant for patients in uncontrollable pain with only six months or less left to live. They claim the Oregon law is successful. However, in the years of Oregon's law, there has not been one documented case of assisted suicide being used for untreatable pain. Instead, patients are using assisted suicide for psychological and social concerns. Since legalizing assisted suicide, Oregonians have seen first-hand what really happens. *When physician-assisted suicide is legalized, safeguards don't work.*

Oregon's Experience

First Case The first known case of physician-assisted suicide was a woman in her mid-80's who had been battling breast cancer for twenty years. Her long-time physician refused to prescribe a lethal dosage; a second physician diagnosed her as depressed and also refused the assisted suicide request. The woman then sought the help of assisted suicide advocates who found a physician willing to prescribe a lethal overdose. The doctor who wrote the lethal prescription knew her two and a half weeks. In a taped conversation with the woman before her suicide, she lamented she could no longer pick her flowers. She added, "I am looking forward to [suicide] because, being I was always active, I cannot possibly see myself living out two more months like this. . . . I will be relieved of all the

A DISPOSABLE SOCIETY

Ramirez. © 1997 by Copley News Service. Reproduced by permission.

stress I have." *A depressed patient was Oregon's first known assisted suicide victim.*

Matheny Case Patrick Matheny was 43 years old and diagnosed with ALS (Lou Gehrig's disease). After obtaining the pills by Federal Express, he struggled with the decision of when to use them. By the time he decided to take the lethal drugs he was unable to adequately swallow and his brother-in-law admitted to "helping" him. It is illegal under Oregon's law for a patient to receive help in suicide. A legal opinion from the Oregon Department of Justice was requested. The Deputy Attorney General answered that it would "seem logical to conclude that persons who are unable to self-medicate" are discriminated against. If the law is judged to be discriminatory, it will open the door to legalized euthanasia. *A patient hardly able to swallow has pushed the boundary lines of assisted suicide to lethal injection by doctors.*

Cheney Case Kate Cheney was an elderly woman diagnosed with an inoperable tumor. When she requested assisted suicide, her daughter felt her first doctor was "dismissive" of the request and sought another doctor. Kate's second doctor ordered a psychiatric evaluation. The psychiatrist found that the patient did "not seem to be explicitly pushing for [assisted suicide]," had difficulty with short-term memory and lacked the "very high level of capacity required to weigh options about assisted suicide," [according to Erin Hoover Barnett]. He refused the suicide request, saying Kate's apparent dementia, combined with pressure from her daughter, made him wonder whose agenda the lethal drug request really was. Kate seemed to accept the refusal, but her daughter became angry. A second opinion from a psychologist resulted in an approval, although she also noted Kate's memory problems and that Kate's "choices may be influenced by her family's wishes, and her daughter . . . may be somewhat coercive." Cheney did not take the prescription right away. It was not until she spent a week at a nursing home that she finally took the lethal prescription. *A patient suffering beginning stages of dementia and under pressure from her family was a known assisted suicide victim.*

Freeland Case In a paper presented at the scientific meeting of the American Psychiatry Association, May 2004, an account of Oregon's sole documented case of assisted suicide was reported. The case of Michael Freeland, a 63-year-old cancer patient, proves that assisted suicide safeguards don't protect patients. Oregon physicians can't prescribe life-ending drugs to a patient with more than six months to live. But Freeland, who was prescribed lethal drugs by an assisted suicide physician, survived nearly two years after receiving a diagnosis of imminent death. Patients must be judged competent to choose suicide, but Freeland's assisted suicide doctor denied the need for a psychiatric evaluation, even though Freeland suffered from known suicidal, even homicidal depression and paranoia. Authorities later judged Freeland incompetent to handle his finances and medical decisions, yet the lethal dose was not removed from his possession. Freeland eventually died naturally without using drugs, thanks to the intervention from volunteers for Physicians for Compassionate Care, who advocated for pain relief and mental healthcare. This care, which relieved his desire for death, was never supplied by the assisted suicide advocates who, once having written the lethal overdose prescription, only wanted to help him die.

Tax-Funded Assisted Suicide in Oregon

In February 1998, the Oregon State Health Commission added assisted suicide to its list of services to be provided under the Oregon Health Plan. Assisted suicide, listed under "comfort care," was now to be paid for by tax dollars for those of low income. *The state has created financial pressures favoring suicide over good care. Assisted suicide is paid for by tax dollars; adequate pain management, adequate living assistance for the disabled and some life-sustaining treatments are not covered.*

Oregon's Failed Experiment

The Oregon Health Division issues a yearly summary of assisted suicide using information derived from prescribing doctors. No supporting documentation or independent evaluation is provided to determine the assisted suicide was performed in accordance with the law. All information is forbidden to inspection.

The Health Division acknowledged that it had no way to "detect doctors who fail to report assisted deaths or commit other violations of the law."

National studies show that among patients requesting assisted suicide, depression is the only factor that significantly predicts the request for death. Sixty-seven percent of suicides are because of psychiatric depression. *By Oregon's seventh year, only 5% of suicide victims received psychiatric counseling.*

Social isolation and concerns about loss of autonomy and control over bodily function were the causes of assisted suicide. Did patients receive adequate information on alternative palliative care? Were concerns about loss of autonomy and other fears adequately addressed? Was the assisted suicide truly the patient's "last resort"?

Oregon's safeguards are illusory. Assisted suicide has spread beyond the type of people it supposedly was reserved for. A shroud of secrecy encompasses the reporting process of assisted suicide. However publicized assisted suicide cases have proven:

- "Doctor shopping" interferes with long-time physician/patient relationships

- Familial pressure may promote suicide

- Assisted suicide will expand to euthanasia

- Patients suffering from depression and dementia are receiving physician-assisted suicide

- Once receiving a drug overdose prescription from a pro-assisted suicide doctor, patients no longer receive concerned medical care, but instead are abandoned to die.

Once assisted suicide is legalized, it becomes impossible to contain. Once assisted suicide is legalized, it becomes impossible to protect the vulnerable and mentally ill. *Once assisted suicide is legalized, it becomes, essentially, death on demand.*

> "Since Oregon's law was implemented there have been no efforts to expand the law beyond its stringent self-administration guidelines."

Legalizing Physician-Assisted Suicide in Oregon Has Not Led to Abuses

Death with Dignity National Center

In the following viewpoint the Death with Dignity National Center (DDNC) presents its rebuttal to the most prevalent arguments against assisted suicide in Oregon, where the practice is legal. In answer to those who say voluntary euthanasia will inevitably lead to nonvoluntary euthanasia, the organization points out that such a result would never happen in Oregon because patients there are in control of the dying process. To counter those who say that if patients' pain were adequately treated physician-assisted suicide would not be needed, DDNC claims that for a small percentage of terminally ill people, pain can never be relieved. The organization also contends that no one in Oregon, including the poor and disabled, are encouraged to ask for aid in dying. The DDNC is an Oregon-based organization, which proposed and helped pass and implement the law permitting assisted suicide in that state.

As you read, consider the following questions:

1. What are the three reasons cited for the success of the law in Oregon?
2. What was the effect of the law on hospice referrals?
3. What reason is given for the need for physician-assisted suicide in other states?

There's a lot of misinformation that ideological opponents of death with dignity would have you accept as fact. Below, we've got their rhetoric and the reality. . . .

The Law Is Not a Slippery Slope

Opponents Say: Oregon's law is a slippery slope toward euthanasia.

The Truth: Oregon's law is specifically written to ensure that terminally ill patients remain in control of their dying process. Since Oregon's law was implemented there have been no efforts to expand the law beyond its stringent self-administration guidelines. The Death with Dignity Center will oppose any such efforts. This law works because

1. It operates within the confines of the doctor-patient relationship;
2. The patient is the driving force in the process, and;
3. [It is] the person who ultimately administers medication.

Opponents Say: Many people are told they have a few months to live but then are still alive years later; the law encourages people to act too soon.

The Truth: Nobody wants to die. The experience in Oregon has demonstrated that the terminally ill people who sought help from a physician to hasten their deaths did so while fighting to make the most of every day. If an extended recovery were possible, that individual would not even think of using the law, as they would want to make the most of the time they've been given. People in extreme situations for whom recovery is no longer possible use the law as a last resort when each day becomes more and more unbearable.

Opponents Say: Outlawing physician-aid-in-dying will prevent it from happening.

The Truth: Physician-hastened dying happens in every state, every day. Laws will not prevent terminally ill patients from seeking an end to their suffering, nor will they prevent some doctors from quietly helping. Laws can only be used to protect patients and physicians by regulating the practice—ensuring no abuse occurs.

Opponents Say: Families will coerce terminally ill loved ones into using the law.

The Truth: The law clearly states that if there is any evidence of coercion the process must be stopped. Physicians, working closely with terminally ill patients and their families ensure that this will not be a concern.

Proper Pain Management

Opponents Say: Proper pain management can alleviate a patient's desire for a hastened death.

The Truth: Even the most ardent opponents of Oregon's law admit that for 5% of terminally ill people even the best pain care will not alleviate their suffering. The sad truth is that the actions of the DEA [Drug Enforcement Administration] means that even the 95% of terminally ill people who could have their pain managed adequately, risk not getting good pain care because doctors will fear DEA investigation. In addition, pain is only one element in this complex problem. For many terminally ill people, it is the loss of dignity and autonomy—the suffering beyond pain—that becomes intolerable.

Opponents Say: People can hasten their deaths through terminal sedation and dehydration just as easily as with Oregon's law.

The Truth: Terminal sedation and dehydration is a legal way to end your life in all 50 states. In this scenario, the patient stops eating and drinking. The doctor provides sedation so that the patient does not feel the effects of starvation and dehydration. The process can take up to two weeks and there is no consciousness due to the excessive sedation. The prescriptions used under Oregon's law usually render the patient asleep within a few minutes and death usually comes within a few hours, if not sooner. You decide which is more humane.

The Law Does Not Undermine Important Health Care

Opponents Say: Hospice utilization will decrease as patients choose assisted dying.

The Truth: In Oregon, hospice referrals and use actually increased to about 32%, almost double the national average and higher than any other state.

Opponents Say: Patients will no longer be able to trust their physicians to do everything possible to cure them.

The Truth: In fact, many people in Oregon are having conversations about this issue with their doctors while still in good health. Doctors in Oregon have done everything their patients have wanted to prolong life, and have been allowed to fulfill some patients' final wishes when suffering became unbearable.

Oregon Law Has Safeguards

[Oregon's] Death with Dignity Act legalizes PAS [physician-assisted suicide], but specifically prohibits euthanasia....

To receive a prescription for lethal medication, the following steps must be fulfilled:

- The patient must make two oral requests to his or her physician, separated by at least 15 days.

- The patient must provide a written request to his or her physician, signed in the presence of two witnesses.

- The prescribing physician and a consulting physician must confirm the diagnosis and prognosis.

- The prescribing physician and a consulting physician must determine whether the patient is capable.

- If either physician believes the patient's judgment is impaired by a psychiatric or psychological disorder, the patient must be referred for a psychological examination.

- The prescribing physician must inform the patient of feasible alternatives to assisted suicide including comfort care, hospice care, and pain control.

- The prescribing physician must request, but may not require, the patient to notify his or her next-of-kin of the prescription request.

"Requirements," Seventh Annual Report on Oregon's Death with Dignity Act, Department of Human Services, Office of Disease Prevention and Epidemiology, March 10, 2005.

Many Oregonians want to know their doctors will not abandon them if their suffering becomes intolerable and will work with them should they decide to choose death with dignity.

The Law Will Not Result in People Taking Their Lives Who Are Not Terminally Ill

Opponents Say: Oregon's law contributes to a "culture of death."

The Truth: Oregon's law has brought peace of mind to many terminally ill patients who more often than not say something like "I don't know if I'll use the law, but knowing it is there as an option gives me the strength to go on." If that's not life affirming, what is?

Opponents Say: Disabled people will be encouraged to use the law.

The Truth: No one is encouraged to use the law. The law is in place for terminally ill people whose suffering is intolerable and who wish a humane and dignified death. The law is rarely used in Oregon but it does supply real comfort to many people who see it as an option—if they need it. There are many disabled people who support the Oregon law.

Opponents Say: The poor, undereducated, uninsured, racial minorities and other marginalized people will be encouraged to use the law.

The Truth: No one is encouraged to use the law. Oregon's experience indicates that the people who chose to use the law are well educated, have had excellent health care, good insurance, access to hospice and were well supported financially, emotionally and physically.

The Law Has Adequate Reporting and Safeguards

Opponents Say: Doctors don't have to report under the Oregon law. Therefore we really don't know how many people have used it or how successful it has been.

The Truth: Doctors cannot qualify for the law's "safe harbor" provisions if they do not report use of the law to the Oregon Department of Human Services [DHS]. A doctor that does not report to DHS would be subject to reprimand.

Opponents Say: Oregon is the only state where physician-aid-in-dying occurs.

The Truth: Every day in every state, doctors are quietly responding to patients' pleas for help in hastening death. The difference in Oregon is that it is done legally, in the open, and it is carefully regulated to ensure the patient, family and caregiver are protected. Oregon's law was written specifically because proponents learned this practice was happening and wanted to make sure it was properly regulated to protect those involved.

Opponents Say: HMOs and insurance companies will encourage people to use the law.

The Truth: These decisions are made between patients and doctors, in consultation with family. No HMO or insurance company is ever involved with these decisions and were they to be, it would qualify as coercion, which is strictly prohibited under the law.

Opponents Say: People will move to Oregon to hasten their death.

The Truth: The law requires terminally ill patients to be residents of Oregon. There is no evidence that anyone has moved to the state expressly to use the law.

The Law Does Not Make People "Play God"

Opponents Say: Dying is a process and Oregon's law circumvents that process and the potential for closure and healing that might occur between the patient and their family or friends.

The Truth: Oregon's experience demonstrates that these processes are not circumvented and that the support of family and friends in the final days is often enhanced. Goodbyes are said and often, family and friends are gathered with the patient when they slip peacefully into sleep. The people choosing to use the law have been facing death for years and are asking to use the law only as a last resort; there is no evidence of anyone "rushing" the process.

Opponents Say: Oregon's law is tantamount to "playing God," only God should determine when we die.

The Truth: Modern medicine has become adept at prolonging life and unfortunately, continues to treat death as a failure. With all the technology and treatment options in healthcare today, it is often only the suffering and death that is prolonged—not a superior quality of life. People who might be stuck in the prolonged suffering of a terminal illness and whose belief systems allow them to choose a hastened death, are no more playing God than the people who suggest that one more procedure, one more pill, one more tube might make the difference. . . .

Federal Laws Do Not Prohibit Death with Dignity

Opponents Say: The Controlled Substance Act (CSA) enables the federal government to overturn Oregon's law.

The Truth: The Controlled Substance Act is a federal law, which governs the trafficking of illegal substances like cocaine, and ensures that narcotics are used for legal medicinal purposes and not diverted for other use. Oregon's Death with Dignity law allows for the legal use of controlled substances and therefore the CSA does not apply. Further, it is the states, not the federal government that determine what is legitimate medical practice. Oregonians determined through two elections and several federal court cases that death with dignity is a legitimate medical purpose, meaning that as long as physicians operate under the law, they are protected.

Opponents Say: The U.S. Supreme Court ruled against physician-aid-in-dying in Oregon.

The Truth: The U.S. Supreme Court refused to hear a challenge to Oregon's law, thus allowing the law to go into effect on October 27, 1997. In two cases argued earlier that year, the court found no federal right to physician-aid-in-dying but encouraged an "earnest and profound debate" about the issue. Furthermore, the Court determined that the issue was more appropriately decided by the individual states. Oregon has made its decision.

> *"My fear is that [assisted death] will be-*
> *come a constant presence in health-care*
> *settings, a big friendly mutt that lays*
> *its head in [the] lap [of the disabled]*
> *and wags its lethal invitation whenever*
> *we doubt our ability to go on."*

Legalizing Voluntary Euthanasia Would Harm the Disabled

Barry Corbet

Barry Corbet, former editor of New Mobility *magazine, suffered a spinal cord injury in a 1968 helicopter crash, leaving him disabled. He was also an author and filmmaker before his death in 2004. He says in the following viewpoint that although he sympathizes with the disabled who ask for help in dying, he opposes the legalizing of the physician-assisted suicide (PAS). Corbet sees too many problems with making PAS legal. For example, he questions the wisdom of granting doctors the power to decide who should be eligible for assisted dying. He also believes that the list of groups and individuals eligible for physician-assisted suicide would inevitably grow, as the criteria that distinguish them would seem increasingly arbitrary.*

As you read, consider the following questions:

1. What two disability-rights organizations does Corbet discuss?

2. What criticisms of the Oregon Death with Dignity law does the author outline?

3. Why does Corbet favor assisted death without the involvement of physicians?

It's so deceptive, this one simple question: Should we make it legal for people to secure a doctor's assistance in hastening death? Yes or no? Ask, and you might get a definitive answer. Ask why, and what you'll get is slippery, contentious, anything but definitive. Yet we hold to our polarized answers and we do, by God, love them. In our crowd, to take a renegade position is to invite our own public beheading. The wise stay out of it. But we can't. Since virtually all people who request hastened death have old or new disabilities, we're essential to the debate. Death-with-dignity laws are about us.

The discord begins with a name—whatever we're going to call death requested by a patient and facilitated by a physician. The most commonly used term is physician-assisted suicide, or PAS. In disability circles, that acronym stands for personal assistance services, so is rejected here. Not Dead Yet, a major player in the debate, prefers physician-induced death, or PID. It has undertones of medical murder so is rejected on the basis of bias. For this discussion, I've compromised with physician-assisted death, or PAD.

Some background: Suicide is legal in every state, as is passively attending a suicide. Euthanasia, actively helping someone end their life, is illegal in every state. PAD, a physician providing a lethal dose for a patient to take without further assistance, is legal only in Oregon. Two disability rights-based organizations have formed to address the PAD question: Not Dead Yet, which opposes PAD and the Oregon law, and AUTONOMY, which endorses both. . . .

In attempting to understand PAD, I've viewed it from three perspectives, each raising progressively harder questions: PAD as personal prefererence, PAD as a disability issue and PAD as public policy. The categories overlap, but they guide us toward asking the right questions. . . .

Physician-Assisted Death as Personal Preference

Faye Girsh [former president of The Hemlock Society, which is now part of compassion and choices] asked me what seems like a reasonable question: "Why can't those who don't want hastened death live out their full lifespans and those who do want it have this humane option available to them?" Girsh meant the question innocently, but is it truly benign? Not if it's the alpha and omega of the discussion. It sweeps way too many valid concerns under the rug, even on a personal level.

You may feel comfortable in your decision that under certain circumstances you want PAD. You've talked to your family, doctor and hospital, and given everyone copies of your advance directives, the legal documents that state your wishes. You've entrusted your medical power of attorney to someone close. But did you know how easily your advance directives, and therefore your life-and-death choices, can change or be completely ignored?

"In an ideal world, advance directives include individual decisions based on personal consultation with a physician," says Lauri Yablick, a Tucson psychologist who works with people with disabilities. "How can there be informed consent without that?"

Yet by law, on admission to a hospital or nursing home, you must be asked if you have, or want to create, advance directives. At each readmission, the question is repeated. That means an untrained clerical worker often solicits a life-or-death decision from a sick or forgetful patient, an uninformed relative or a court-appointed guardian. Just sign the orange form, honey, and we'll get you in bed.

"Each new admission brings the potential for a surrogate decision-maker to override the pre-existing directive," Yablick says. "I've found inconsistent advance directives on more charts than you can imagine. And the options are pared to a dichotomy. No matter what your advance directive says, your chart says 'full code' [save me no matter what] or 'DNR' [do not resuscitate]. No one's considering clauses like 'meaningful chance for recovery.'" We should find this unsettling. If advance directives can change, how can we have PAD and feel confident that we're following the person's wishes?

But you're a take-charge person, you can make things happen your way. Or can you? You may be unconscious when the time comes, or demented, declared incompetent or taken to an unfamiliar hospital. Your appointed surrogate may have died or your doctor retired. Dozens of things can change, and you aren't in charge anymore.

And how realistic are our ideas of what is acceptable health in the future? "Before your accident would you, fairly, have been able to protect yourself into the life you've led since your injury?" Yablick asks. Not a chance. We may say we are not willing to live with certain physical or mental states, but do we really know what we're afraid of? Sometimes the fear is disproportionate to the reality. . . .

Physician-Assisted Death as a Disability Issue: Those Against It

Here's another reasonable-sounding question, this time from the late Drew Batavia: "Disability rights are about autonomy and self-determination. Why shouldn't that freedom of choice extend to end-of-life decisions?"

Because, NDY [Not Dead Yet] might say, the current state of institutionalized prejudice against people with disabilities turns that choice into no choice. Because nondisabled people seem to fear disability more than death. Because doctors are fallible in diagnosing and treating depression and estimating life expectancy. Because the current rush to cut health-care costs conflicts with our need for lifelong care. Because PAD can be seen as the ultimate sanction, the ultimate form of discrimination.

Our PAD "choices" may, in fact, be subtly conditioned. "The problem is that our desires are so malleable and manipulable," says Harriet McBryde Johnson, a disability rights attorney from Charleston, S.C., and a supporter of NDY. "You know how easy it is to internalize other people's expectations, how exhausting it can be to oppose them, especially when you're sick. What we confront usually isn't homicidal hate, it's that pervasive assumption that our lives are inherently bad. That attitude can wear us down to the point where we want to be killed."

Can't we build ironclad safeguards into the law?

"Safeguards as presently proposed," counters Johnson, "are about defining a class whose desire to die may be presumed rational, because of illness or disability so 'bad' that no 'reasonable' person would want to endure it. That whole veneer of beneficence. The law has the power to validate and structure prejudice. These [PAD] laws tell suicidal newbies that yes, it really is as bad as it feels, and don't expect it ever to get better. They tell the larger society that disability and illness equal misery, so there's no need to bother about making our lives good. There's an easy way out."

Johnson acknowledges the possibility of individual situations where assisting a suicide or looking the other way might be morally right. "But I wouldn't try to objectively define those situations and build law around them," she says. "It just can't be done. Killing is too serious to manage by checklist."

And what of our physical vulnerability? "We are living the lives that others fear," says Johnson. "I depend on others to keep me alive every day. If I'm lucky, I get them to honor my requests—and keep me alive—on the strength of my paychecks and my charms. But money and charms are transient and, at bottom, we need people to know they're stuck with us no matter what and that they'll see us through those days when we feel bad about the pressures we put them under or when we get tired of all the complications."

With PAD, insurers may be less inclined to see us through. As a class, we're both poor and expensive; beer income, champagne needs. We're the medically unattractive. Of course we fear that insurers will deny us expensive treatment options while holding out the carrot of "a peaceful and dignified death." The cheapest care is no care.

If eligibility for PAD is based on health status, then what is health status? It's a construct grounded in the medical model, and doctors are its arbiters. Yet doctors have a singularly vivid sense of how rotten our lives are. According to several studies, they underrate our quality of life and overestimate our depression, and those perceptions do affect the treatments they prescribe and the advice they give. Given both PAD and prospective payment, will they be too quick to write us off?

We may help them do it. All it will take is one sympathetic health-care worker reporting our ambivalence, however momentary, about staying alive. Then the wheels can turn, doctors can agree that our lives are unendurable, and we can be hustled off to hospice amid a nauseating chorus of people saying we're dying the way we wanted to. With absurd ease, we can be put out of our "misery" with no malice on the part of any segment of the health-care system. It happens now. Is this freedom of choice?

Physician-Assisted Death: Those for It

We are not a right-to-die group, wrote Drew Batavia, the president of AUTONOMY until his death in January [2003]. "We are a disability-rights organization that supports our right to decide issues of our lives. The unifying theme is choice and control."

Batavia and Hugh Gallagher co-founded AUTONOMY partly to fight Attorney General John Ashcroft's efforts to nullify Oregon's Death With Dignity Act, partly as a reaction to NDY. Batavia felt that while the leadership of many disability-rights groups opposes PAD and presumes to speak for all of us, many of the rank and file support it.

He may be right. In a 2001 Harris Poll, 68 percent of people with disabilities polled nationwide favored PAD. A small study by Pamela Faden shows a fairly even split, but she warns against using her survey to quantify consensus. Her study does show that many members of disability-rights groups fear criticism if they speak out in favor of PAD. . . .

"Assisted suicide," [Batavia] wrote, "cannot be held responsible for the consequences of our society's failure to provide adequately for the needs of many people with disabilities." Jack Kevorkian? "Kevorkian demonstrated why laws like the Oregon Act are necessary. He operated without standards." People with nonterminal conditions? "I admit to some ambivalence about this issue," Batavia wrote in 1999, but he included only terminal conditions when speaking for AUTONOMY. And always, Batavia returned the discussion to choice. "Our overall mission," he said, "is to provide a full range of options for people with disabilities." And elsewhere: "Our positions are based fundamentally on the value of autonomy." . . .

Do the Oregon law's guidelines, as Johnson suggests, simply define a class considered better off dead? "Absolutely not," Gallagher says, "The Oregon law is reactive, not proactive. . . . It has the support of a large majority of its citizens. It's an insult to say Oregonians believe their terminally ill loved ones are better off dead. It cheapens and polarizes a serious moral issue."

Gallagher is not looking for conflict. "This is not a game of one team opposing another. Different people, cultures and religions hold different positions. These positions must be respected. AUTONOMY believes it should be up to the individual. Our whole purpose is to reduce the vulnerability of disabled persons to outside influence. We are grown-ups and we don't need Ashcroft telling us what we can or cannot do."

And Gallagher sets out his own credo: "I have fought hard to live my life as I choose to live it, to make my own life decisions. I will not give up this autonomy of decision making on my deathbed.". . .

Physician-Assisted Death as Public Policy

Most unassisted suicides tend to be grotesque. They're violent or fail or create new disabilities. They exclude loved ones at a time when closure is needed. Wouldn't the option of PAD be better than that?

"I think it ought to remain difficult and messy," says Harriet Johnson, "something you'd think about pretty hard before doing. I don't see every suicide as irrational or even tragic. However, I have no trouble following NDY in toto when it comes to the law, which is what NDY is really about. Killing should remain a criminal act. When it's discovered, we should prosecute. But the law isn't the same as justice and never will be. It serves too many conflicting purposes to represent any kind of ideal.". . .

[There is] another sticky question: Johnson thinks Oregon's restriction of its PAD law to people with six months to live is suspect. "It's really illogical to give them, and only them, the right to a quick and easy out. I agree with Kevorkian that if anyone 'needs' death services it's people with a long life expectancy who are miserable. I don't quite understand why the lines are drawn the way they are. But then, I reject the whole idea of line-drawing.". . .

"I believe that whether or not to continue living is as personal a choice as anyone could make," says Lauri Yablick, "and that helping people die is potentially as valid a role for health-care providers as helping them live." But legalizing PAD? "No. Not here, not now, and given our health-care system, not for a long time. This is such a complicated issue and people want to treat it so simply."

Yablick questions the Oregon law's lack of consistency and inclusion. "The Oregon Act excludes most people with mental conditions. Who sold the myth that we can make a clear, reliable and objective determination of competency and emotional stability? Where's the logic in excluding people with depression and other serious mental illness—groups with the highest rates of suicide—from the sanctioned version? Won't people with progressive dementias still feel pressured to act prematurely? Who decided that physical suffering trumps emotional suffering?

"Another great fallacy is that regulations prevent abuses," she says. "[The] Ten Commandments didn't bring a loving and peaceful world. More laws didn't bring fewer prisons. And the regulations intended to prevent other health-care abuses have failed miserably. I know in every finger, toe and split end that widespread acceptance [of PAD] will result in further abuse."

Yablick points to how easily health professionals can encourage someone to die. "The way I see this playing out if PAD is added to the mix is that, in the midst of an outburst, some disinhibited pain-in-the-ass substance-abusing patient exclaims, 'I'd just rather be dead!' He suddenly gets the individual attention he's been craving in this understaffed pit, and is lovingly coached to his rightful place.

"The law has to be crafted for the most vulnerable members of society," Yablick reminds us. "The law is for everybody. How can we support hastened death under these circum-

Pressured to Die

The disabled are among the most discriminated-against people in our society. Many disabled people are poor and must rely on Medicaid, resulting in their often experiencing profound difficulties gaining access to quality medical care. Frequent studies have shown that lack of adequate health care can lead to suicidal ideation. Moreover, disability-rights activists report that the value of disabled patients' lives are so discounted by some medical professionals that they are sometimes pressured to sign do-not-resuscitate orders (DNRs)—even when being treated for non-life-threatening conditions.

It is in this context that the disability-rights community almost unanimously opposes legalizing assisted suicide/euthanasia.

Wesley J. Smith, "A 'Doctor Death' Runs for President," National Review Online, September 4, 2003. www.nationalreview.com.

stances? It's a choice I want available for me and for everyone I love, but it's just too damn costly."

Assisted Death, Not Physician-Assisted Death

The law is for everybody. Viewed through that framework, some of the pieces shift into place and some go skittering off the puzzle board. What you make of PAD is your business, but here's where I landed after I made it mine:

After all the discussion, suicide remains a personal matter. Individuals, not organizations, commit suicide. We shouldn't moralize or psychologize after the fact.

Suicide aided by laypeople who provide knowledge and support . . . raises the ante. More people participate and coercion, by others or by circumstance, becomes a greater concern. Yet Hemlock [The Hemlock Society, now called Compassion & Choices] and other programs like it provide an alternative to PAD, and perhaps a better one. They enable facing death peacefully in the home, after the goodbyes are said, with friends and family present.

If we really want the option of hastening death, and if Hemlock were to drop its advocacy for PAD and concentrate on what it already does—take the P out of PAD—I'd be tempted to say it's the best way we can provide some autonomy in end-of-life decisions without opening the door to systemic abuse.

True, utilizing Hemlock's help can send a terrible message about disability, but it's a gentler message than legalizing PAD. And what message do we send if we allow ourselves to linger through intractable pain, dementia, through it all, whatever we've got, into nothing? Won't people say, "I wouldn't want to die that way"? Is it so bad to end a good life with a good death?

PAD is an enormous escalation from suicide, either solitary or in the company of others. It makes our end-of-life choices the province of law, medicine and economics, as implemented by a deeply flawed health-care system. My fear is that PAD will become a constant presence in health-care settings, a big friendly mutt that lays its head in our laps and wags its lethal invitation whenever we doubt our ability to go on.

Readers with long memories may recall that I've been kinder to PAD in the past. I said I wanted the option available for myself and couldn't bring myself to distrust my doctors or hospitals. I feel the same now, but was wrong to think my preference was relevant to PAD legislation. It's relevant only to me.

Arguments Against Legalization Prevail

NDY's arguments do seem relevant. They no longer strike me as paranoid and shrill, but as reasoned reflections of horrors already seen. With all my faith in my health-care providers, I have seen them. And NDY, more than other organizations, addresses the complexity of the issue.

AUTONOMY's arguments are tight, attractive and easy to grasp. That's its strength and its weakness—all its philosophical eggs in one basket. Personal autonomy is a worthy goal, but it's only one factor in lawmaking and, for that matter, disability rights. It offers no guarantee of benefit to society.

In the diffuse light of complexity, I see PAD inviting excess—eugenics resurrected by fetal DNA testing, for example, or [Philip] Nitschke's vision of one-way euthanasia cruises, burial at sea included. Kevorkian's posturing as a savior. Peter Singer's promotion of infanticide for disabled newborns.

I'm left with too many inconsistencies that smell fishy. Why limit PAD to people who are terminal? Don't the nonterminal suffer? Why is PAD wrong in the presence of depression? Is it not part of the suffering that needs relief, and must we disqualify anyone whose depression cannot be cured? Why a waiting period for PAD requests? Whose asses and assets are we covering? Why offer PAD to people who are physically capable of taking their own lethal dose, and deny it to those who are not? Why aren't we better at the long-term and palliative care that might make PAD less attractive? Why do we "respect" the suicidal wishes of disabled people, yet treat the same wishes of nondisabled people as cries for help? Why would we make trusted doctors speed our passage to eternity? Why do so many people want PAD only because they're afraid of becoming like us?

There are good answers to some of these questions. But until they all, and many more, are part of the debate, we don't understand the issue.

There may come a time when PAD will make sense in this country. I cautiously hope so. But PAD now? I don't think so.

"*[Arguments made by the disabled] fail to show that legalization of [physician-assisted death] would introduce any new risks that are not already present in current policy.*"

Legalizing Voluntary Euthanasia Would Not Harm the Disabled

David J. Mayo and Martin Gunderson

David J. Mayo and Martin Gunderson contend in the following viewpoint that although the disabled make convincing arguments against physician-assisted suicide (PAS), their claims fail to make the case against legalization. For example, opponents cite horror stories in which disabled patients are encouraged to die against their wishes simply because they are disabled. However, the authors point out that these abuses occur in the present regime, where PAS is illegal. Mayo and Gunderson maintain that this argument merely supports the view that existing laws against discrimination should be enforced to stop the abuses they were designed to prevent. Laws could also be enforced to prevent similar abuses should PAS be legalized, they claim. David Mayo is a professor at the University of Minnesota and has served on the boards of the Hemlock Society and the National Death with

Dignity Center. Martin Gunderson is a philosophy professor at Macalester College in Minnesota.

As you read, consider the following questions:

1. What rationale was used in the court case *Canterbury v. Spence,* according to Mayo and Gunderson?
2. Why do the authors say that the arguments of disability advocates fail as a case against legalization of physician-assisted death?
3. In what two ways can protective policies err, according to Mayo and Gunderson?

All are not equal when it comes to access to health care. Members of vulnerable populations, and especially those who suffer prejudice, face severe barriers in getting decent health care. These barriers are a central topic in bioethics. But the problem can itself get misused. Some bioethicists have opposed physician-assisted death (PAD) on the ground that it poses special risks to the vulnerable. These arguments have found their way into policy: government task forces and courts, including the supreme courts of the United States and more recently of the State of Alaska, have adduced concern about the vulnerable either to oppose PAD or to uphold state laws proscribing PAD.

The Importance of Risk-Based Arguments

Particularly important are the risk-based arguments against PAD given by advocates for persons with disabilities, such as Not Dead Yet and Americans Disabled for Attendant Programs Today (ADAPT). They merit attention for several reasons. First, they rest on well-documented discrimination against persons with disabilities. It is in large part because of such discrimination that persons with disabilities are vulnerable and in need of special protections. Second, they are representative of arguments raised on behalf of other groups that are vulnerable to prejudice.

Third, and perhaps most important, they now play a prominent role in the public policy debate about legalizing PAD. . . . Because these arguments link the possible risks of legalizing PAD with the actual abuses suffered by persons with severe disabilities as they seek the health care to which they are entitled, and because those who advance them often speak both *for* and *as* persons at risk, they have proven to be particularly effective criticisms of PAD.

The arguments raise serious concerns regarding the medical care of persons with disabilities. At a minimum, they indicate a need for greater sensitivity on the part of health care workers and for better protective regulation in all areas—not just end of life decisionmaking. When directed specifically against PAD, however, they fail to show that legalization of PAD would introduce any new risks that are not already equally present in current policy. More importantly, they presuppose a form of vitalism that is incompatible with the current policy of informed consent governing medical decisionmaking, even in end of life cases. The link to vitalism is the more remarkable since the arguments given by disability critics of PAD often appeal explicitly to concerns about informed consent.

The Demise of Medical Vitalism

Virtually everyone holds that human life has extraordinary value. As dramatic life-prolonging technologies were developed in the middle of the twentieth century, this conviction gave rise to the aggressive use of these technologies whenever they held the promise of prolonging life. . . . By the 1960s the prevailing practice had come to be one of aggressive application of life-prolonging technologies whenever they held a promise of delaying death. We refer to this policy of prolonging life whenever possible as medical vitalism. . . .

Medical vitalism came not only to guide medical practice, but also to provide the basis for much early criticism of the notion that terminally ill patients should be informed of their prognoses so that they could make informed decisions about further life-prolonging therapy, advance directives, hospice, and of course euthanasia and PAD.... The paternalism that dominated medical practice until the 1960s was not mere authoritarianism. It often meant aggressive end of life care motivated by medical vitalism.

Our purpose here is not to argue against medical vitalism, nor against the philosophical doctrine behind it. We take it as a given that the policy has lost currency in the past thirty to forty years. Certainly many Americans, above all those with loved ones who have suffered painful deaths, are quick to agree that protracted terminal illness can sometimes mean a fate "worse than death." In any event, explicit appeal to medical vitalism is now rare among critics of PAD. Two major developments have contributed to its demise: the dawning of the realization that these new medical technologies sometimes do more harm than good, and the renunciation of medical paternalism in favor of the doctrine of informed consent....

Throughout the 1960s and 1970s, medical paternalism had waned and given way to the doctrine of informed consent as a result both of case law and of federal regulations regarding human subjects research. The classic case of *Canterbury v. Spence,* for example, held that mere consent for medical treatment was not sufficient and that the consent needed to be informed by knowledge about facts that would influence a reasonable patient. The court's rationale was based almost wholly on the right of the patient to determine what happens to his or her body. In particular, patients should be able to determine for themselves when to refuse proposed treatment....

The doctrine of informed consent is typically justified by appeals to individual autonomy, understood as self-determination. Hospice and proposals for advance directive

The Rights of the Disabled

We do not believe that the right to assisted suicide is premised on a diminished quality of life for people with disabilities. It is based on respect for the autonomy of terminally ill individuals during their final days. . . . We further contend that, though we must always be vigilant in preventing abuses, the right will not necessarily be expanded to individuals or situations for which it was not intended. . . .

We believe that abuses of assisted suicide, to the extent they are now occurring behind closed doors, are less likely to continue once assisted suicide is legalized and appropriately regulated.

Andrew I. Batavia, "Disability and Physician-Assisted Dying," in Physician-Assisted Dying in the Case for Palliative Care and Patient Choice, 2004.

legislation were reviled for challenging vitalism when they were first proposed in the 1960s and early 1970s. Today all states have advance directive statutes, the federal government has endorsed such efforts with the Patient Self-Determination Act, and the courts have affirmed the right of patients to refuse even life-saving treatment. Hospice care is now widely recognized as the gold standard for end of life palliative care. . . . Current standards of end of life care now allow the administration of palliative drugs in whatever doses are required for adequate pain control, even if those doses may hasten death, just so long as the hastening of death is not intended, but merely foreseen.

In short, vitalism has now yielded to patient self-determination as the guiding principle in end of life decision-making. Indeed, respect for self-determination is so deeply rooted in our moral and legal thinking that advocates for persons with disabilities often invoke it in defending laws such as the Americans with Disabilities Act and in arguing for increased access for persons with disabilities. Against the background of this shift, critics of PAD have increasingly relied on risk-based arguments rather than on medical vitalism.

Vulnerability Related Arguments Against PAD

Those who argue that vulnerable patients might be subjected to PAD without their genuine consent broach a variety of concerns. Members of vulnerable groups might be coerced into PAD either directly, by others who are prejudiced against them, or indirectly, by having only unjustifiably restricted options available to them. Alternatively, they might make inauthentic choices because they have internalized others' oppressive opinions about them. Such arguments appeal to the moral importance of self-determination. Thus at first blush they seem to be in line with the shift in the past three decades to the policy of informed consent that emphasizes patient self-determination. . . .

Representative arguments appear in the *amici curiae* brief to the Supreme Court filed by Not Dead Yet and ADAPT in connection with *Vacco v. Quill.* All of the arguments in the brief proceed from general claims that society fears and is repulsed by disability and that these attitudes engender pervasive discrimination and prejudice. Many of the arguments arise specifically from the claim that abled Americans tend to believe that they (and by implication anyone) would rather be dead than have to live with a serious disability. Even caregivers of persons with disabilities share this prejudice and routinely underestimate how highly clients with severe disabilities value their own lives.

The brief also illustrates the prejudice's dire consequences. DNR orders may be routinely issued for persons with severe disabilities entering health care facilities. Many members of

Not Dead Yet and ADAPT report having been "repeatedly requested and pressured to sign DNR requests." One disabled person who used a ventilator was told as she entered a health care facility that she would be assigned a DNR status even after she made it clear that she demanded otherwise. In another case, health care providers allegedly sought authority to withhold treatment contrary to directives from both the patient and family. . . .

The brief cites four celebrated cases of non-terminally ill persons with severe disabilities who tried to end their lives by refusing life-prolonging therapy. When caregivers unwilling to accommodate these patients sought court orders permitting them to continue treatment, the courts ruled in each case that the patients' requests must be honored. Thus, disability critics argue, the courts themselves are inclined to deny persons with severe disabilities the "equal protection" of standard suicide-prevention measures, and instead "demonstrate that prejudice, stereotypes, and devaluation of people with disabilities have already had a substantial adverse impact on members of this minority group.". . .

When those who are subject to such discrimination internalize values from the dominant culture, an even more insidious problem arises. Advocates worry that those who internalize the oppressive group's disvaluing of their lives may come to regard themselves as a burden when they need medical care. Thus they argue that legalization of PAD might make people opt for death not to spare themselves pointless suffering, but to spare others from bearing the burden of caring for them. About a third of those who have died over the past four years [1998–2001] under Oregon's Death with Dignity Act have cited concerns about being a burden to family, friends, or caregivers. The International Task Force on Euthanasia and Assisted Suicide construes such statistics as evidence that "the right to die will become a duty to die." The underlying concern is that persons with disabilities who choose PAD because they believe themselves to be a burden have simply internalized prejudice and are therefore not choosing authentically. . . .

Another manifestation of deep-seated discrimination against vulnerable groups is that they may be denied options and opportunities that are available to others. In the context of health care, some may lack access to treatments that others can obtain. Lacking treatment options, somebody might choose PAD because it's the best of the remaining options. . . .

In light of all these considerations, disability critics of PAD argue that no possible set of safeguards could provide disabled persons adequate protection against coerced and other mistaken physician-assisted death. In the words of the brief from Not Dead Yet and ADAPT. "cloaked in the false rhetoric of 'personal autonomy,' physician-assisted suicide threatens the retaining rights of a profoundly oppressed and marginalized people."

Medical Vitalism Revitalized

Disability advocates paint a profoundly disturbing picture of a world in which severely disabled Americans must struggle against fear and prejudice, even within the health care system. Let us accept these horror stories at face value. Many require no ethical analysis. They call instead for corrective measures ranging from improved safeguards to a change in the ethos both of the health care system and of the culture generally.

These arguments fail, however, *as a case against the legalization of PAD.* They fail because all of the risks of premature death they enumerate are already risks of current policy, as articulated by the doctrine of informed consent even in connection with end of life decisions (by advance directive if necessary). The cases cited are "horror stories" precisely because they involve monstrous violations of current policy. Health care workers should never assume that a severely disabled patient would opt for a DNR classification. The other cases described in the brief depict even more egregious violations of existing policy. It is difficult to imagine how any health care facility could seek "to withhold treatment in opposition to express patient and family directives to the contrary." All of these represent clear abuses of existing policy, which quite properly allows refusal of treatment by fully informed, competent patients.

Similarly, even if we agree that the reasoning was prejudiced in the four celebrated cases in which courts refused to override the state suicidal wishes of persons with severe disabilities, the courts' mistakes were not hypothetical mistakes that *might* have resulted from the legalization of PAD, but *actual* mistakes in the implementation of current policy on the right to refuse treatment. Indeed, the brief even describes these as "right to die cases," and speaks of the parties in question as committing suicide. This hardly seems evidence for the view that "holding the line" against legalizing PAD could serve in any way to minimize premature deaths. The fact is that current law is on the side of any competent American who chooses to end his or her life not only by refusing "medical" life-prolonging therapies, but by simply abstaining from food and drink.

Strengthen Safeguards for Informed Consent

Current policy with respect to medical decisionmaking is deeply committed, morally and legally, to self-determination and the doctrine of informed consent. Terminally ill patients who have decided that enough is enough and want to die (along with terminally ill patients who want state-of-the-art palliative care) are currently legally enticed to refuse life-prolonging therapies. Indeed, laws proscribing assault and battery are ultimately on the side of any competent American who elects to end his or her life simply by no longer taking food or drink. In embracing this policy, society has accepted the risk of some premature deaths—risks we try to minimize with appropriate safeguards. The arguments advanced by disability critics of PAD make a compelling case for strengthening these safeguards, particularly for patients with disabilities. They have failed to show any *additional* risks to patients who may already opt to cut short a fate they view as worse than death. Indeed, the safeguards that accompany Oregon's "right-to-die" law are clearly *more stringent* than those that apply to cases in which terminal patients routinely elect to forego life-prolonging therapies, often in the context of electing hospice care.

If these arguments against PAD are persuasive, they also provide strong reasons for rejecting current policy requiring informed consent. There are two alternatives for those who find these risks unacceptable; they can either press for improved safeguards in the implementation of the current policy on informed consent, or they can press for a policy in which considerations of self-determination are overridden by considerations of preserving life—in short, by medical vitalism. Not Dead Yet and ADAPT adamantly deny, however, that the risks they cite could be adequately addressed by safeguards. In effect, then, they argue for a return to medical vitalism. It is ironic that the powerful arguments they and others make about the need to protect the consent process of those who are vulnerable to prejudice should, when applied specifically to PAD, actually undermine the foundations of informed consent. This is a far more radical implication than is currently recognized, even by critics of these arguments. . . .

Risks and Policies

Protective policies addressing risk are ubiquitous: FDA drug licensing procedures, traffic laws and driver requirements, even parental policies governing the expanding liberty of their teenagers, all aim to protect against the risks of mistaken or abusive exercise of liberty by restricting it. Protective public policies themselves, however, also run risks. Strong safeguard policies risk limiting justifiable action, while weaker, more permissive safeguards risk harmful misuse of liberty. Thus protective policies can err in either of two directions: they may either fail to provide adequate protection against actions that turn out to be harmful, or they may restrict action that would have been beneficial.

Protective policies governing end of life decisionmaking are no exception. On the one hand, there is the risk of premature death, which critics of PAD have emphasized but which is already implicit in the current policy of informed consent. On the other hand, there is the risk of a prolonged or delayed death that only adds a period of extended pointless suffering while denying an individual control over his or her final days. To "err on the side of life," after all, is to *err*. Ronald Dworkin argues that this error must be taken seriously: " forcing people to live who genuinely want to die causes serious damage to them." The danger of this error presumably explains why most Americans favor the legalization of PAD.

Yet disability critics of PAD seem to dismiss the risk of this error out of hand. They merely point to the possibility of premature death, as if this consideration trumped. Their claim that adequate safeguards are impossible seems to imply that any "adequate" safeguard would be a perfect safeguard. Because they deny that better but less-than-perfect safeguards could reduce the risks to acceptable levels and because the risks they cite are risks equally present in the current policy on informed consent, this amounts to a de facto commitment to medical vitalism—the policy most protective against the error of premature death but least respectful of individual self-determination. . . .

Self-Determination Is Core Value for Disabled

A return to vitalism, however, would not only be completely at odds with our current, deep commitment to the doctrine of informed consent. It would be equally at odds with a primary goal of the disability movement generally. . . .

Clearly the ADA [Americans with Disabilities Act], which greatly expands protections for persons with disabilities in employment, public services, and public accommodations, generally has as its purpose the promotion of self-determination, in the broad sense of both controlling one's own private life and fully participating as a citizen in the life and governance of the community. Indeed, it is difficult to see how the protections afforded by the ADA could be understood independently of the value of self-determination.

Clearly, too, the ADA reflects the goals of the disabilities movement in general. The ADA was influenced by proposals drafted by the National Council on the Handicapped in 1986. In addition, intense lobbying by advocates for persons with disabilities, as well as a variety of public hearings at which persons with disabilities had a voice, went into the drafting, and passage of the ADA. The ADA's emphasis on self-determination is not new, but is reflected in previous federal legislation protecting persons with disabilities from discrimination, including the Rehabilitation Act of 1973 and the Persons with Disabilities Education Act of 1970.

There are many within the disability community *advocating* for PAD precisely because of their commitment to the goal of increased independence and self-determination for people with disabilities. In an *amici curiae* brief filed in connection with *Washington v. Glucksberg,* disability advocates of PAD note that "[i]ssues of autonomy and self-determination are at the heart of the struggle of people living with disabilities. They want to be able to control the decisions that affect their lives." The brief concludes that "the fundamental right of self-determination must apply to all significant life decisions, including what is perhaps the most intimate and personal decision of all, whether to hasten impending death if their conditions become terminal and they are suffering intolerably.". . .

PAD critics who are reluctant to sacrifice self-determination in favor of vitalism must either come forward with new arguments alleging additional risks that would be introduced by the legalization of PAD, or abandon their claim that it poses unacceptable additional risks. Indeed, if they are concerned chiefly with the risk of premature death among vulnerable populations, they might press this concern as an argument for improving safeguards in connection with current end of life policy. . . .

Arguing in favor of PAD as an implication of respect for the self-determination of persons with disabilities would in no way discount the legitimate concerns about the abuse of persons with severe disabilities at the hands of their caregivers. But it would redirect the response toward finding better safeguards, in connection with medical decisionmaking for vulnerable populations generally.

Periodical Bibliography

The following articles have been selected to supplement the diverse views presented in this chapter.

Drew Batavia and Hugh Gregory Gallagher	"An Open Letter to People with Disabilities," Independent Living Institute, 1999. www.independentliving.org.
Raphael Cohen-Almagor	"Non-voluntary and Involuntary Euthanasia in the Netherlands: Dutch Perspectives," *Issues in Law & Medicine*, Spring 2003.
Diane Coleman	"Disabled Group Objects to 'Dignity' of Assisted Suicide, Doubts Motives," *Rocky Mountain News*, March 19, 2005.
Stephen Drake	"Euthanasia Is Out of Control in the Netherlands: Changing the Rules to Accommodate Bigotry," *Hastings Center Report*, May/June 2005.
Chris Feudtner	"Control of Suffering on the Slippery Slope of Care," *Lancet*, April 9, 2005.
Marilyn Golden	"Why Assisted Suicide Must Not Be Legalized," Disability Rights Education and Defense Fund, 2003. www.dredf.org.
Karen Hwang	"Attitudes of Persons with Physical Disabilities Toward Physician-Assisted Death: An Exploratory Assessment of the Vulnerability Argument," *Journal of Disability Policy Studies*, June 22, 2005.
Hallvard Lillehammer	"Voluntary Euthanasia and the Logical Slippery Slope Argument," *Cambridge Law Journal*, November 2002.
National Right to Life Committee	"A Dose of Sober Realism in Oregon," *National Right to Life News*, June 2004.
Debra J. Saunders	"Death with Vanity," *San Francisco Chronicle*, January 4, 2005.
Stephen W. Smith	"Fallacies of the Logical Slippery Slope in the Debate on Physician-Assisted Suicide and Euthanasia," *Medical Law Review*, Summer 2005.

CHAPTER 4

When Should Life
Support Be Stopped?

Chapter Preface

Medical practices that would have been deemed unacceptable fifty or even twenty years ago have now become nearly commonplace. The withdrawal of a respirator or food and fluids from a comatose patient, for example, would not have taken place in 1950. However, a 1976 lawsuit made the withdrawal of life support legal, and widespread acceptance of the practice followed. In the *Quinlan* case the parents of a comatose woman, Karen Ann Quinlan, wanted to take her off of a respirator, but the hospital refused. The parents were ultimately victorious, and their daughter was removed from the respirator. She continued to live nine years longer with only food and fluids as treatment. Most people now view the removal of life support as "letting die" rather than "killing," and therefore do not see it as a form of active euthanasia. However, not everyone agrees, and controversies over the practice still occur.

Today, as long as the family is in agreement, patients in a persistent vegetative state (PVS) can be taken off of respirators and feeding tubes. Media attention is usually only generated in the case of disagreement among family members, as in the high-profile 2005 case of Terri Schiavo. At twenty-six years old, Schiavo suffered an anoxic brain injury, and was diagnosed as being in a PVS. Her husband maintained that Terri would not want to live in her current state, and he eventually requested that her feeding tube be removed. Her parents disagreed and fought in court against the removal. After years of legal battles, and despite the intervention of Florida governor Jeb Bush and the U.S. Congress, Schiavo's feeding tube was removed, and she died thirteen days later in March 2005.

Schiavo's situation was contentious primarily because her wishes were not clearly expressed before her injury, and she could not give consent for the removal of her feeding tube. It was difficult to tell whether either her husband or her parents were in fact complying with what Schiavo would have wanted. The attention led to a flood of requests for living wills and other advanced directives. Some people wanted to specify that they would want to have feeding tubes removed if they were in Schiavo's condition. Others wanted to assert that they would want food and water if they became incapacitated. Many more people have now discussed their wishes regarding end-of-life care with loved ones so that their families do not have to go through the ordeal suffered by Schiavo's.

As the ending of life support has become more acceptable, Americans are taking steps to make their medical wishes known. The following viewpoints examine when it is appropriate to remove life support, and whether living wills are an effective way to make sure that a patient's wishes concerning life support are respected.

"If we know that the heart stopped beating, and they develop this what we call 'wakeful coma,' which is a persistent vegetative state, we know they're never going to recover."

Feeding Tubes Should Be Removed from Patients in a Persistent Vegetative State

John Collins Harvey

John Collins Harvey is a senior research scholar and professor emeritus of medicine at Georgetown University. In the following viewpoint Harvey argues that feeding tubes should be removed from patients in a persistent vegetative state. According to Harvey, these patients will never recover because their cerebral cortex—the area of the brain that controls mental functioning—has been destroyed due to a lack of oxygen. Keeping such patients alive places an undue financial burden on patients' families and society, he contends, pointing out that the money could be spent on patients who have hopes of recovery.

As you read, consider the following questions:

1. What example does Harvey give of times when a feeding tube is mandatory?

John Collins Harvey, "Interview: Dr. John Collins Harvey," *Religion & Ethics Newsweekly*, Public Broadcasting Service (PBS), May 21, 2004. Copyright © 2004 by *Religion & Ethics Newsweekly*. Reproduced by permission.

2. How does Harvey feel about not putting in a feeding tube when someone has a brain injury?

3. What are several factors the author lists for consideration when a family is deciding whether or not to remove a feeding tube?

*A*s *both a moral theologian and a physician, do you make a distinction between keeping someone alive on a respirator and keeping someone alive on a feeding tube?*

John Collins Harvey: No, and that's a very misunderstood thing. What's important to understand is certain illnesses cause pathological conditions so that an organ system does not work—let's say kidney disease, and certain kidney diseases will destroy the total function of the kidneys in the body. We can substitute now a machine that does the physiological work of the kidneys. That's renal dialysis machines. And people with kidney disease who would otherwise have died can remain alive being dialyzed maybe two or three times a week and they can go on, for many years, living.

The same situation occurs when people have difficulty breathing. We have a machine that will breathe artificially for somebody. So we put a tube down their trachea, attach it to the machine, and it will do the breathing for them. We have the ability to have an artificial heart that will do the work of the normal heart when the heart has failed. The point is that if you can do, substitute the physiological mechanisms artificially for those that have failed, we use that. If the situation is a fatal, pathological condition that can never, ever be overcome, then one has to look at the boons and the benefits of this artificial, physiological mechanism.

Reasoning Behind Use of Feeding Tubes

Why is a feeding tube, in your view, the same as keeping someone alive on a respirator or through dialysis, and not elementary comfort care?

Because if it's being done where there's fatal pathology, it is just as if you were using the kidney machine on somebody who has no kidneys. They can stay alive, but if they decide that they don't want to undergo this, it's too much of a burden, it's perfectly moral to stop.

When somebody has a condition in which they can never bring food to their mouth by use of their arms; they can never chew food if it's placed in their mouth, because the muscles of mastication are paralyzed; if they can never move the bolus of food that they have put in at the front of the mouth and then moved by the tongue back to the esophagus, where automatic peristalsis takes place, and down the food goes to the tummy and then is absorbed and whatnot—if that is a fatal pathology that they never will recover, the ability to chew and swallow, then if we use administration of food and fluid artificially, we're prolonging biological life. We're not prolonging an individual to where cure can take place, and then we remove that artificially administered fluid. Just because it's such a simple machine, such a simple tool, it makes it no different from a respirator, from an artificial heart, or from kidney dialysis machines.

The best way I can explain that is if an individual has what we call a tetanus infection, which is caused by a bug, an organism that grows in a small wound anyplace on the body, and it produces a poison, tetanus toxin, and the tetanus toxin affects all the muscles of the body, but particularly the muscles of mastication. It's known as "lockjaw," because as it advances, it makes the mouth clench. The body is stretched so that the person forms an arc because the back muscles are very tense and tight. We can treat the wound where the bug is growing and putting tetanus poisons into the system by antibiotics, like penicillin. Over a period of a month, we can get rid of that wound, overcome the infection; and the effects of the toxin gradually wear off, so that the individual will be able to recover fully the ability to eat normally. If we did not use a tube to feed that individual during this time of terrible physiological defect, he or she would die, because they would get no nutrition. So it would be mandatory to feed this type of individual.

But in the persistent vegetative state, there is no hope ever of recovery of this normal physiology of eating, swallowing, and giving food to yourself.

What is "fatal pathology," in the medical view?

It's a pathology brought about by a disease process that can never be cured and is going to ultimately lead to the individual's death.

Causes of Persistent Vegetative State

How do you decide that someone is truly in a persistent vegetative state?

We know the ability for an individual to express what we call his or her personhood—to love, to think, to remember, to talk, to move is all done by the biological substrate in the brain called the cerebral cortex; that's the upper part of the brain. The lower part of the brain controls the vegetative activities of the body, like making sure the heart is beating at its given time, that we're breathing regularly, that the kidneys are making urine, that the bladder is being able to fill it up and then expel the urine through the urethra. These are all vegetative activities in the body which we're not even aware of.

The cerebral cortical cells and the vegetative area of the brain—if they are deprived of oxygen for given periods of time, they will die. The cerebral cortical cells can only tolerate the lack of oxygen for about six minutes, and then they die. And the death is irreversible, and no new brain cells ever grow up. Over a period of time, the cerebral cortex degenerates, disintegrates, and it just becomes in the skull kind of a bag of mush. The vegetative cells in the lower part of the brain can withstand the lack of oxygen for 40 to 50 minutes, and they will continue to function.

All of the cells of the body can be deprived of oxygen for different periods of time. The fingernails, for instance, can still metabolize and whatnot without being supplied by oxygen for a period of 24 hours. The kidneys also can work deprived by oxygen, so that very often people that are pronounced dead because their heart stops and their respiration stops—the bladder will be filled, will have urine accumulated in it after death has been pronounced because the kidneys are still doing a little work. The death of cells is at a different time rate after oxygen has stopped being circulated, which means the heart has stopped beating and the lungs are not aspiring so that oxygen is supplied to the blood. In the persistent vegetative state, the individual has been without blood going to the head for at least six minutes, so the cerebral cortical cells have died. How does this come about? It comes about because the heart stops beating. The heart can stop beating from a heart attack, from a coronary occlusion. The heart can stop beating if the individual is electrocuted by lightning on the golf course. The heart will stop beating if the individual is drowned. And sometimes, the heart will stop beating when there's a terrible severe trauma to the head. The heart does not stop beating when an individual is poisoned by drugs and is put into a permanent coma by a drug, like the [Karen Ann] Quinlan case. Severe trauma does not always make the heart stop, but it can discombobulate the cells of the cerebral cortex, so that we see people who are in coma for 10, 15 years, and very rarely you will hear they woke up one day. That's because they are not in the persistent vegetative state, because they did not have cessation of oxygen going to their brain at any time during their illness. But individuals who have had that, and the oxygen has not gotten to the brain over that period of time that I described—they are never going to recover, because they do not have any brain cells to recover. Brain cells that are discombobulated by drugs, alcohol, or by a trauma—their physiology is just disrupted, but maybe over 20 years it finally returns to normal.

Does it always happen that way? Are there exceptions to the rule?

Well, I do not think that we can talk about people who appear to be in the persistent vegetative state where we know that their heart has not stopped beating. But if I know that the heart has stopped beating, that the heart was started up at the scene of the accident by the emergency medical technicians, who can revive individuals now, get their heart going, get them reanimated—if we know that the heart stopped beating, and they develop this what we call "wakeful coma," which is a persistent vegetative state, we know they're never going to recover.

If the history is one of drug intoxication, or trauma, where there's no record that the heart has stopped beating, then I do not think that we can say that's the persistent vegetative state. That's persistent coma. I think we have to be careful about withdrawing food and fluid from those people. . . .

Families That Do Not Want to Remove Nutrition

What do you say, as an ethicist, to the family that just will not give up hope, even given the medical facts, that their relative will come out of this, will recover?

You give them the medical facts that their relative can never recover if they're in the persistent vegetative state, and so doing these things is futile treatment. As a physician, I could not ethically give futile treatment to a patient. That's wrong.

The Benefits of Dehydration and Foregoing Tube Feeding	
Effect on Body	*Benefit*
Less fluid in the lungs	Easier to breathe
Less fluid in the throat	Less need for suctioning
Less pressure on tumors	Less pain
Less frequent urination	Sheets can be changed less frequently Less risk of skin breakdown and bedsores
Increase in the body's natural pain-relieving hormones	Increased comfort and less pain

Joanne Lynn Harrold and Joan Harrold, *Handbook for Mortals*, 1999.

What do you say to the family that will not remove that tube?

I would talk to the family very carefully, point out all of the issues, and then say, "You know, I, in conscience, cannot continue this treatment because it's futile. The individual is dying." The burdens of such treatment are so great, compared to the benefits—the benefits are maintaining purely biological life. I would say to that family, then, "I can't continue to be your doctor because I do not believe you're doing the right thing by this patient. I think it's poor medicine. It's a poor way of treatment. And I feel I'm a good doctor and try to do the best for my patients."

Now, this is purely the medical aspects of things. I'm not talking anything now about the moral aspect. This is if any patient came to me, regardless of his or her religion, and insisted that we continue feeding a person in the persistent vegetative state as I have defined the persistent vegetative state. If they would not follow my medical advice, I would have to ask them to find another doctor to take care of their patient, which is the correct way physicians deal with individuals. You never abandon a person, but you help them find another doctor who will work the way the family wants. . . .

What do you say to those who believe that a feeding tube is really comfort care, elementary care of a person; it is not an extraordinary measure.

But it is an extraordinary measure because of the fatal pathology. Many individuals who insist it is comfort care simply do not understand the complexities of which I have been talking. And many of these people are very adamant and very zealous in their insistence, but they just have not understood the teachings of the [Roman Catholic] Church with these nuanced kind of changes. . . .

Making Decisions About Removing a Tube

When a family is making a decision to put in a feeding tube, what types of considerations should go into that decision?

I think the diagnosis has to be quite clear. In my opinion, the way I treat patients, I would never consider taking a feeding tube out of anyone who was in permanent coma or who developed, then, the wakeful coma that is fairly characteristic of the persistent vegetative state. I, personally, would not even talk about removing it until a year had passed.

Why is it such a turning point, putting that tube in?

Well, it's not a turning point. We use it all the time for pathology that prevents somebody from taking in food. It's perfectly good and useful and mandatory care, as I said. If somebody has tetanus infection, you would be committing a mortal sin, you would be committing a felony against that person if you did not use a feeding tube.

What about cases where there has been some deprivation of oxygen to the brain?

If the history is so clear as that would be, then I would, after six months, when they're in the persistent vegetative state, feel it's perfectly okay to withdraw the feeding tube.

But what about putting the feeding tube in, to begin with?

I would never not put the feeding tube in, because I think it's one of those things that you never know. A miracle may occur. The individual may wake up. We may have made a misdiagnosis. The heart may not have stopped, but people thought it did.

Is there a time that you would say, "Well, we should give up hope at this point"?

A year. Absolutely.

The Cost of Care

How expensive is it to keep someone alive on a feeding tube?

It's about $60,000 to $80,000 a year.

How do you weigh the costs and benefits of this?

The cost-benefit is entirely moral to consider; that is one of the burdens that the family or the community is bearing. And if the community feels that it can't afford that benefit for patients in Medicare, or if a family feels, with its private funds, it has a limited amount of money to send the grandson to college or to keep Grandma alive in a nursing home in this futile situation, the cost can be considered a burden. The psychological burden of the family, the terrible psychic trauma of seeing this individual, their loved one, lying in this condition for over a year is very, very costly on the psyche

of family members. That can be brought into consideration. Pius XII said that. Gerald Kelly, a great Jesuit priest who was a great medical moralist, said that way back in the '50s.

Given the huge costs of keeping someone alive on a feeding tube, do you think families might be susceptible to pressure to remove their family member from the feeding tube in that case?

I can give you an instance of that. There was a family that had just such a situation. The patient was transferred to a nursing home, and the individual's insurance provided for something like four or five months' care in a nursing home, which most hospital insurance doesn't provide for chronic care. They were insistent that the tube be kept in until they found they had a burden to keep it in—namely, $60,000 a year.

Would it be moral to remove it in that case, when money is the only burden? Is cost a valid moral basis upon which to make your decision?

Cost is a burden. The moralist Gerald Kelly and Pius XII both said that extraordinary burdens do not have to be borne by patients or families or communities, and cost is a burden to be considered in maintaining an individual in a persistent vegetative state with a feeding tube. . . .

How about government intervening in these cases [when there is disagreement about removing a feeding tube]?

I do not think government should intervene. If the physician is doing the best he or she can do, is following the best medical, moral practices, I do not think there should be intervention in the doctor-patient relationship. That does not mean that people can do things that are illegal. But I'm just saying that a very excellent doctor who's following his or her best ability to give the right care to an individual, following all

that we've been taught from both the physical, scientific and moral standpoint, should not be interfered with by outside bodies.

Burdens of Maintaining Care

If you were making the decision to remove the feeding tube, could you tick off some of the points that people should look at?

How much nursing care is required? Is it taking nursing care from other people who need it and would benefit by it? And there are physical and medical complications which are a burden that an individual would not be forced to undergo. Then you have to think of the burden to the family next. Is the terrible psychic trauma that can occur—the disruption of normal family relationships, with fighting going on between different members of the family arguing "yes," "no," "yes," "no," can be terribly disruptive and destroy a whole family this way. The psychological burden on the family, the financial burden on the family. And then the financial burden on the community. When you spend $60,000 a year on taking care of somebody and the care is not going to bring them back to a cognitive life, but merely maintain biological life, is it wise, if their community resources are of a given amount, to use them this way, or to use them for benefit of many more people in a different way?

When you say the burden on the community, you mean that Medicare generally pays for all of this.

Absolutely—Medicare or Medicaid. It might be that money can be used to a much better advantage in the care of citizens where the care given is going to have an effect on the outcome of that disease or illness that the patient has, or preventive medicine measures, whereas, the care that we give to these people—loving care, expensive care—is not going to have any effect, except maintaining biological life. . . .

| "New categories of people are now the victims of discrimination and exploitation."

Feeding Tubes Should Not Be Removed from Patients Diagnosed as Being in a Persistent Vegetative State

Wesley J. Smith

Wesley J. Smith argues in the following viewpoint that feeding and hydration tubes should not be removed from those who are diagnosed as being in a persistent vegetative state. He takes issue with the use of "vegetative" to describe brain-damaged persons, arguing that many patients diagnosed as such are not dying and could eventually recover so long as feeding and hydration continue. Moreover, removing tubes from these patients is cruel, for they feel the pain associated with hunger and thirst, he maintains. Smith is an attorney, a highly visible anti-euthanasia advocate, and the author of numerous books including Culture of Death: The Assault on Medical Ethics in America, Power over Pain, *and* Forced Exit: The Slippery Slope from Assisted Suicide to Legalized Murder.

As you read, consider the following questions:

1. According to the author, what is the difference between

Wesley J. Smith, "Dehydration Nation," *Human Life Review,* Fall 2003. Copyright © 2003 by the Human Life Foundation, Inc. Reproduced by permission.

the two circumstances in which nourishment is withheld?

2. Why does Smith disagree with using the label "persistent vegetative state"?

3. What court decision does the author cite as establishing
a two-tiered system of constitutional rights?

For more than ten years, conscious and unconscious cognitively disabled people who use feeding tubes have been legally dehydrated to death in the United States. This intentional life-ending act—clamping feeding tubes and denying all
sustenance—has become so ubiquitous that, generally, little
attention is paid.

This public indifference was shattered by the Terri Schiavo
litigation [in 2005], an epic legal, political, and media struggle
that pitted Terri's parents, Bob and Mary Schindler, against
her quasi-estranged husband, Michael Schiavo. At stake was
whether Terri would live, as fervently desired by her parents,
or die by dehydration as demanded by her husband. . . .

The Schiavo case is not the first "food and fluids" case, but
it is certainly the most notorious. Widespread revulsion over
Terri's court-ordered dehydration sparked a grass-roots political campaign that culminated in the Florida legislature's
rushed passage of "Terri's Law," which empowered the governor to intervene and prevent some categories of cognitively
disabled people from being dehydrated. As soon as the bill became law, Governor Jeb Bush dramatically halted Terri's dehydration in its sixth day, setting off an international uproar. . . .

Difference in Circumstances for
Withholding Nourishment

At this point we must distinguish between two different circumstances in which nourishment is withheld from incapacitated patients:

- First, not forcing food and water upon dying patients

who reject nourishment. This often occurs in the end stages of cancer. Indeed, it is recognized as *medically inappropriate* to force-feed patients whose bodies are shutting down during the natural dying process. In these cases, the patients die from their disease, not dehydration. *This is not the situation that this article addresses.*

- Second, withholding tube-supplied food and water from cognitively disabled persons like Terri *who are not otherwise dying.* In such cases, nourishment is withheld not for medical reasons but because someone believes that the patient's life is not worth living in such an impaired state, or that he or she would rather be dead than live with a profound cognitive disability. Death in these situations is caused by dehydration.

If the owner of a horse or cow caused the animal to die by withholding food and water, he or she would probably go to jail, and rightly so. If a condemned murderer were executed by being shut in a room without food and water until he died, the American Civil Liberties Union would never stop suing, and rightly so. (Ironically, the ACLU has jumped into the Schiavo case—on *Michael's* side, to have Terri's Law declared unconstitutional.) But dehydrate a person with significant brain injury who requires a feeding tube, and it is considered medically ethical, the right to refuse unwanted medical treatment and an adjunct of the legally non-existent "right to die."

A Potentially Painful Death

Advocates for dehydrating the neurologically disabled assert that it is a painless end. But there are substantial reasons for doubt. St. Louis neurologist Dr. William Burke told me:

A conscious person would feel it [dehydration] just as you or I would. They will go into seizures. Their skin cracks, their tongue cracks, their lips crack. They may have nosebleeds because of the drying of the mucus membranes, and heaving and vomiting might ensue because of the drying out of the stomach lining. They feel the pangs of hunger and thirst. Imagine going one day without a glass of water! Death by dehydration takes ten to fourteen days. It is an extremely agonizing death.

Minnesota neurologist Dr. Ronald Cranford, an avid supporter of dehydration, who has often appeared as an "expert witness" in litigation over withholding food and water, testified in the Robert Wendland case about the effect of dehydration on cognitively disabled patients:

> After seven to nine days [from commencing dehydration] they begin to lose all fluids in the body, a lot of fluids in the body. And their blood pressure starts to go down. When their blood pressure goes down, their heart rate goes up .... Their respiration may increase and then ... the blood is shunted to the central part of the body from the periphery of the body. So, that usually two to three days prior to death, sometimes four days, the hands and the feet become extremely cold. They become mottled. That is you look at the hands and they have a bluish appearance. And the mouth dries a great deal, and the eyes dry a great deal and other parts of the body become mottled. And that is because the blood is now so low in the system it's shunted to the heart and other visceral organs and away from the periphery of the body. . . .

Case of Kate Adamson

Since the people to whom this is done generally can't communicate, we mostly don't know what they actually experience. But in at least one case we do: that of a young woman who had her tube feeding stopped for eight days and lived to tell the tale.

At age 33, Kate Adamson collapsed from a devastating stroke. She was diagnosed as likely to develop a persistent vegetative state (PVS) but was actually "locked in"—that is, she was completely awake and aware but unable to communicate.

Even after the doctors realized that Adamson was entirely conscious, they urged her husband to "let her go." He refused, and indeed, when she developed a bowel obstruction, he authorized surgery. However, to clean the bowel enough to permit surgery, her nourishment was stopped. When, eventually, she recovered her ability to communicate, she wrote *Kate's Journey: Triumph over Adversity.* Appearing on *The O'Reilly Factor,* Adamson described the experience of being denied nourishment:

> When the feeding tube was turned off for eight days, I thought I was going insane. I was screaming out in my mind, Don't you know I need to eat? And even up until that point, I had been having a bagful of Ensure as my nourishment that was going through the feeding tube. At that point, it sounded pretty good. I just wanted something. The fact that I had nothing, the hunger pains overrode every thought I had.

In preparation for an article in the *Daily Standard,* I asked Adamson to provide more details about what she experienced while being deprived of tube-supplied nourishment. As an illustration, she told me that she was administered inadequate anesthesia during her bowel-obstruction surgery. Yet, as painful as that was, it *was not as bad* as the suffering caused by being denied nourishment:

> The agony of going without food was a constant pain that lasted not several hours like my operation did, but several days. You have to endure the physical pain and on top of that you have to endure the emotional pain. Your whole body cries out, "Feed me. I am alive and a person, don't let me die, for God's sake! Somebody feed me."

Moreover, although Adamson was not deliberately dehydrated—she was constantly on an IV saline solution—she *still* had horrible thirst. . . .

Doctors who withhold nourishment and hydration with the purpose of causing death may prescribe morphine or

"Persistent Vegetative State" Is Bad Terminology

[Dr. Bryan] Jennett and [Dr. Fred] Plum's 1972 naming of post-coma unresponsiveness as "persistent vegetative state (PVS)" characterised the condition as essentially irrecoverable and insentient. The evidence for these propositions was always weak, and they have been largely disproved by more recent research. Nonetheless, the definition and the attitudes it embodies remain generally accepted, resting as they do on a firm foundation of medical attitudes to disability and a public willingness to evade uncomfortable facts. The first step in altering our approach to people with this form of communication impairment must be to rectify our understanding of the terminology.

C.J. Borthwick and R. Crossley, Neuro Rehabilitation, 2004.

other narcotics to alleviate the pain. But who knows whether this is sufficient? For example, when Cranford was asked during his Wendland testimony what level of morphine would have to be given to prevent the patient from suffering, he testified that the dose would be "arbitrary" because "you don't know how much he's suffering, you don't know how much aware he is. . . . You're guessing at the dose." He added that he would probably put Robert Wendland back into a coma to ensure that he did not feel pain!

The Human "Non-Person"

Why do we tolerate such an apparently cruel method of life termination? First, it is an unfortunate by-product of the legal right to refuse unwanted medical treatment. Tube feeding is deemed medical treatment—rather than humane care that cannot be withdrawn—because a modest surgical procedure is required to insert the tube. Thus, even though there can only be one result—death—tube-supplied nourishment can be withdrawn like any other medical procedure. (Many people believe erroneously that there is a legal difference between "extraordinary care," such as a respirator, which can be withheld, and "ordinary care," such as tube feeding, which must be provided. The law recognizes no such distinction.)

Second, when a patient is incapacitated, decisions to accept or refuse medical treatment must be made by surrogates. This means that someone other than the patient will decide whether a cognitively disabled patient lives, or dies by dehydration.

The great Christian bioethics pioneer Paul Ramsey, author of the seminal book *The Patient as a Person*, worried presciently that surrogate decision making could endanger the lives of people who were seen as devalued. Thus, while Ramsey believed that people should be allowed to refuse treatment for themselves on a subjective quality-of-life basis, he urged that decisions made on behalf of others be strictly based on medical needs. Otherwise, he wrote, we could be shifting "the focus from whether *treatments* are beneficial to patients to whether patients' *lives* are beneficial to them."

If bioethics had adhered to the sanctity/equality of life ethic advocated by Ramsey, we would today have far fewer worries about the way cognitively disabled and frail elderly people are cared for in our nation's hospitals and nursing homes. Unfortunately, the academic philosophers who now dominate bioethics shifted the predominant ideology of the field sharply away from the Ramsey approach and toward the "quality of life" ethic. This measures the moral value of human lives subjectively based on levels of cognitive capacity. Thus, most bioethicists today distinguish between "persons" and so-called human "non-persons," people denigrated on the basis of their low level of cognitive functioning.

These invidious distinctions matter very much in the medical setting. Being categorized as a non-person is dangerous to life and limb, since most bioethicists assert that only persons are entitled to human rights. In the full expression of personhood theory, non-persons are killable, subject to the harvesting of their body parts, and candidates for non-therapeutic medical experiments. . . .

Having closely observed many food-and-fluids cases over the last ten years, I have noticed several patterns and themes that, I believe, tell us quite a lot about the state of our culture and, if you will, our national soul.

Personhood Theory Has Successfully Dehumanized the Cognitively Impaired

None of us should have to earn our personhood. Indeed, the foundational philosophy of our country, so eloquently expressed in Thomas Jefferson's "self-evident" truths, holds that we all are equally possessed of inalienable rights, the first of which is the right to life. And while it is certainly true that the United States has too often failed to live up to the soaring ideals of our founding, at least we have struggled mightily and at great cost to overcome the vestiges of our unequal past and make the blessings of liberty available to all.

But with the coming of personhood theory, new categories of people are now the victims of discrimination and exploitation. This is epitomized by the popular use of the profoundly dehumanizing pejorative "vegetable" to describe cognitively disabled people. Once their moral worth has been reduced to that of a cucumber, it becomes easier to justify their killing.

These attitudes are especially dangerous in the medical setting. The medical profession has even picked up the common slur and given it a clinical sound—persistent vegetative state (PVS). Patients diagnosed as being permanently unconscious—PVS—can almost never be saved from dehydration once the primary caregiver decides to stop tube-supplied sustenance, *even* if close family members object. Moreover, there is serious advocacy at the highest levels of the medical intelligentsia for allowing doctors to refuse *wanted* treatment for such people on the basis of quality-of-life determinations. Some even urge that doctors be allowed to kill them for their organs.

Relative Value Should Not Be Placed on Humans

The law, which should be especially vigilant in defending those who can't defend themselves, instead generally reflects the dominant view in bioethics that relative value can be placed on human lives. In this milieu, the greater a patient's capacities the more legal protection he or she receives. Thus, Robert Wendland and Michael Martin[1] were spared dehydration despite "expert" bioethics testimony that they should "be allowed" to die precisely because they exhibited just enough cognition to make the high courts uncomfortable with terminating their lives. Had they been less responsive, it is unlikely that they would have been spared.

Proof of this concern can be found in the California Supreme Court's Wendland decision, which established a two-tiered system of constitutional rights—one for the conscious and another for the unconscious—by explicitly excluding patients diagnosed with PVS from its protective terms. This led to the surreal ruling that Californians lose some of their constitutional rights if diagnosed with PVS, but then regain them if they unexpectedly awaken. Thus, despite its good news for conscious disabled people, *Wendland* is actually a very dangerous decision because it implicitly applies personhood theory to—and thus discriminates against—specific class of born human beings.

1. These men were both severly brain damaged in automobile accidents. Their spouses went to court to attempt to remove artificial feeding tubes.

Casual Statements Can Become a Dehydration Warrant

Those who wish to dehydrate the cognitively disabled invariably claim that they are doing it *for* the patient—that they are doing what the patient said he or she would want done in the event of serious illness or incapacitation. Yet, because the benefit of the doubt in law and culture now tacks overwhelmingly in favor of death in these cases, it is shocking how often the most casual statements have been treated as if they had been carefully deliberated upon advanced medical information.

It has even gotten to the point that courts may hold disabled people to past statements that they would want to die over present indications that they want to live—as the trial judge in Michael Martin's case did.

The worst of these cases of which I am aware is the tragic dehydration of Marjorie Nighbert. Marjorie was a successful businesswoman until a stroke left her disabled. She was unable to swallow safely, but not terminally ill. She was moved from Alabama to a nursing home in Florida where she would receive rehabilitation to help her relearn how to chew and swallow without danger of aspiration. A feeding tube was inserted to ensure that she was properly nourished during her recovery.

Marjorie had once told her brother Maynard that she didn't want a feeding tube if she were terminally ill. Despite the fact that she was *not* dying, Maynard believed that she had meant that she would rather die by dehydration than live the rest of her life using a feeding tube. Accordingly, he ordered all of Marjorie's nourishment stopped.

As she was slowly dehydrating to death, Marjorie began to beg the staff for food and water. Distraught nurses and staff members, not knowing what else to do, surreptitiously snuck her small amounts. One staffer—who was later fired for the deed—blew the whistle, leading to a hurried court investigation and a temporary restraining order requiring that Marjorie receive nourishment.

Circuit Court Judge Jere Tolton appointed attorney William F. Stone to represent Marjorie and gave him twenty-four hours to determine whether she was competent to rescind the general power of attorney she had given to Maynard before her stroke. After the rushed investigation, Stone was forced to report that Marjorie was not competent *at that time.* (She had, after all, been intentionally malnourished for several weeks.) Stone particularly noted that he had been unable to determine whether she had been competent at the time the dehydration commenced.

With Stone's report in hand, Judge Tolton ruled that the dehydration should be completed! Before an appalled Stone could appeal, Marjorie died on April 6, 1995.

Conflicts of Interest Don't Matter in Dehydration Cases

Court-appointed guardians and conservators owe their wards the highest loyalty. As fiduciaries, they are duty-bound to serve their ward's interest—even above their own. Needless to say, among other matters, this means that a guardian cannot personally benefit from financial decisions made while managing a ward's money.

Life is more important than money. Surely, then, the legal prohibition preventing guardians from making monetary decisions when they have conflicts of interest should apply doubly when the guardians would personally benefit from their wards' deaths. Unfortunately, in the food-and-fluids cases, judges have been generally indifferent to these considerations. Even in the face of clear conflicts of interest, judges have seldom been willing to transfer guardianships from those who seek court authority to dehydrate patients to parents or siblings who want their disabled loved ones to live....

Re-humanizing Cognitively Disabled People

Utilitarian bioethicist Peter Singer has written that the food-and-fluids cases are a wrecking ball shattering the sanctity/equality-of-human-life ethic as the first principle of our culture. As much as I hate to admit it, he has a point. Still, to paraphrase Mark Twain, reports about the demise of our traditional human values are greatly exaggerated. The remarkable public outpouring in support of Terri Schiavo's life proves that at least among the general public, the sanctity-of-life ethic retains much of its vitality.

This may show us a way out of our societal miasma. In my more optimistic moments, I see Terri's sweet smile rallying us to reject the views of those who would force us each to earn our personhood by possessing sufficient cognitive capacities and to move instead toward a revitalized society in which every one of us is loved unconditionally as the fully equal and unequivocally human brother or sister that each of us really is. We can do this in the medical setting if we abide by the wisdom of Paul Ramsey and treat every patient "as a person." The first step toward achieving this end is for us all to acknowledge: There is no such thing as a human vegetable.

> "We ought to demand a lot from our healthcare institutions, but that they provide extremely expensive care to the physical bodies of long-gone non-persons. . .is too much to ask."

Doctors Should Stop Treatment That Is Futile

Kevin T. Keith

In the following viewpoint Kevin T. Keith argues that a doctor or hospital has the right to withhold or discontinue treatment for a patient if the treatment would be medically futile—that is, if its benefit to a patient is likely to be little or none. However, conflict can arise, Keith notes, when a family wants treatment for a loved one despite the fact that the treatment would be futile. In these cases, he contends, hospitals have every right to withhold or withdraw treatment if the patient's family is not able to pay for them. The money and resources needed for these treatments are better spent on patients who will benefit from them, concludes Keith. Kevin T. Keith teaches ethics at the City College of New York.

As you read, consider the following questions:

1. What distinction does Keith make between when a patient would have little benefit and when a patient cannot benefit?

2. What is the major reason a hospital will continue to provide treatment to a patient in futile situations, according to the author?

3. What does Keith say is the best management of a situation of conflict?

[There] is a growing spate of stories about hospitals moving to terminate care of patients unilaterally—i.e., against the patients' or families' wishes—when the cases appear hopeless and the patients, have "run out of money." ... There are, naturally, stories about a tragic photogenic infant and a kindly old "grandfather" whose wife weeps "I'm so ashamed of my state that it executes civilians without criminal history."

Decisions Must Be Made About End-of-Life Care

What all these cases have in common is the need to make decisions over "end-of-life care"—treatments provided in the last stages of life, when recovery is known to be impossible. At one time, it was standard practice to provide aggressive care in all cases until the patient was dead. (The obvious inadvisability of this in many hopeless cases was handled informally by hospital staff who agreed among themselves, without consultation with the patients, that certain patients would be "allowed" to slip away.) The suffering this brought to many patients was addressed in the first so-called "right to die" cases, resulting in landmark Supreme Court rulings that patients could refuse "extraordinary" treatments, and finally refuse any treatments they did not personally approve of, and then further that patients could make their wishes known ahead of time in writing (leading to the use of "living wills"), and finally that any convincing evidence of patients' desires—including oral statements to witnesses . . .—could be used as evidence of the patient's wishes, and taken as guidance in determining whether to continue treatment under conditions of severe debility. . . . Gradually a right to refuse treatment not in accordance with one's wishes was developed and—to some degree—promulgated through the legal system.

But not everybody wanted to limit end-of-life treatment. Some patients, or their families, wanted aggressive treatment up to the very end—which, in some cases, could be a very long time. Where the patient had at least minimal brain function, this made sense: though patients have the right to refuse treatment under those conditions, they also have the right to request it if they feel such a life would still be valuable or meaningful to them. (This raises severe problems when the patient's ability to use up caregiving services exceeds their ability to pay for them, and the patient is receiving minimal benefit from them, but in practice most hospitals and nursing homes have tried not to refuse care in those circumstances because it leads to bad publicity. They suck up the cost and write it off.)

However, there is another conflict that sometimes arises: that in which a patient or patient's family demands aggressive or intensive treatment that *cannot* benefit the patient in any significant degree. This may be a demand for an expensive treatment they've heard of that isn't really appropriate for the patient, or a demand for an experimental treatment that shows no promise of working, or a demand for continued treatment for a patient who has no conscious experience at all. (In the latter case, such a patient may not be literally "brain dead" because "death" is a legal concept; not all states accept loss of brain function as a criterion for death, and among those that do, all consider a patient "alive" who has *any* brain function, including merely reflex brainstem functions such as breathing and involuntary muscle movement. Thus, those patients cannot be legally declared dead even though they have no conscious awareness and possibly no upper brain functions at all. . . .) In these cases, distraught or unrealistic family may de-

Ethical Obligations and Futile Care

What are the ethical obligations of physicians when an intervention is clearly futile?

The goal of medicine is to help the sick. Physicians have no obligation to offer treatments that do not benefit their patients. Futile interventions are ill advised because they often increase a patient's pain and discomfort in the final days and weeks of life, and because they can expend finite medical resources.

Although the ethical requirement to respect patient autonomy entitles a patient to choose from among medically acceptable treatment options (or to reject all options), it does not entitle patients to receive whatever treatments they ask for. Instead, the obligations of physicians are limited to offering treatments that are consistent with professional standards of care.

World Federation of Right to Die Societies
"Questions and Answers: Medical Futility" www.worldrtd.net.

mand continued treatment even when it is known that the treatment they are requesting cannot help the patient, or even, as in the case of higher-brain death, when *no* treatment can produce any difference in outcome. . . .

Futility and Scarce Resources

Cases in which a given treatment cannot produce any benefit are known as cases of "medical futility." In some cases, caregivers agree to provide futile treatments simply to avoid the impression of cutting the family off without hope, or to give the family time to come to terms with the reality of the case. But there are other times when that's not a reasonable option. One is when there is excess demand for a certain resource. When a family demands scarce resources, such as access to a necessary piece of equipment that other patients also need and can benefit from, a conflict arises and caregivers try to manage that in favor of the patient who can benefit—but for the family in denial or clinging to unrealistic hope, that solution is not satisfactory. It feels like their family member has been "sacrificed" (because of course they do not agree that the treatment would be "futile"). Another conflict may arise when a patient needs very expensive ongoing treatments—such as intensive life-support—but has no hope of recovery. When a family is willing to pay for this treatment and no conflicting need on the part of other patients exists, most institutions will agree to continue providing the treatment. When the family cannot pay, and the treatment cannot benefit the patient, institutions are much less willing to continue to pay out of their own pockets for intensive care that serves no purpose other than to show the family that something is being done. This smacks uncomfortably of cutting off healthcare simply to preserve profitability, but when the patient has no consciousness or personality and no hope of regaining any, it is a lot more understandable. We ought to demand a lot from our healthcare institutions, but that they provide extremely expensive care to the physical bodies of long-gone non-persons, simply because the former patient's family will not come to terms with the situation or harbors some unrealistic religious belief, is too much to ask. Aside from the question of profit, that money can be spent providing resources and services to other patients. And so, in these cases of clear futility where a family demands ongoing expensive treatment that they cannot pay for, something has to be done.

Cautiously, institutions began to craft policies and seek guidance on handling such conflicts. The best management, of course, is to help the family see reality, both for their own peace of mind and so they will be willing to end the useless charade of treatment for a non-person. When the conflict persists, however, institutions have begun to seek ways to end treatment unilaterally—seeking authority to determine that they will not provide free care forever in "futile" cases.

> *"American medicine now teeters on the edge of a dangerous utilitarian ethic ... 'Any life-honoring value system we still have might succumb to economic pressure.'"*

Doctors Should Not Deny Wanted Treatment

Lynn Vincent

In the following viewpoint World *magazine features editor Lynn Vincent argues against the practice of doctors discontinuing treatment that they consider medically futile. Although doctors claim that such treatments will not benefit the patient and will only prolong death unnecessarily, the real reason, Vincent believes, is that they simply want to save the hospital money. Vincent contends that this approach to treatment is reflective of a broader health ethic that devalues human life.* World *is a weekly newsmagazine written from a Christian perspective.*

As you read, consider the following questions:

1. What states does Vincent cite as having passed laws that allow doctors to withhold or deny wanted treatment?

2. What is the procedure for a family wishing to override a doctor's decision not to provide care?

3. What general principle was established in the 1960s and

Lynn Vincent, "When All's Futile," *World Magazine,* May 21, 2005. Copyright © 2005 by *World Magazine.* Reproduced by permission.

1970s regarding medical decisions, as stated by the author?

On April 21, a British judge rejected the pleas of Darren and Debbie Wyatt who had fought to keep their 18-month-old daughter Charlotte alive. Doctors say Charlotte, born three months premature, is brain-damaged, in continual pain, and likely terminal. Her parents say she can see and hear to a limited extent, and sometimes smiles. While London High Court Justice Mark Hedley agreed that the baby responds to loud noises and tracks the movement of a colorful toy, he upheld an order that would allow doctors to let Charlotte die if she stops breathing.

"I am quite clear that it would not be in Charlotte's best interests to die in the course of futile aggressive treatment," Justice Hedley said.

Welcome to the world of "medical futility," a term that is part real-world health care, part bioethical babble, and wholly at the root of some of the most controversial medical cases making headlines today.

Changes Because of Schiavo Case

Terri Schiavo's death[1] trained public attention on "end-of-life" issues, particularly the importance of making one's wishes known concerning life support, nutrition, and lifesaving by "heroic means.". . .

Brightening legal lines around such issues may be Mrs. Schiavo's legacy, one perhaps more bitter than sweet. But another issue—who decides whether patients like her, those unable to speak for themselves, live or die—is growing less clear. Increasingly, some medical experts point out, clinicians rather than families or surrogates are deciding patients would be better off dead.

1. Terri Schiavo died in March 2005 after a bitter legal battle between her husband, who wanted to disconnect her feeding tube, and her parents, who wanted her to live. Schiavo had been in a persistent vegetative state for 15 years.

The pendulum of medical ethics is "now swinging toward a willingness to consider certain lives not worthy to be lived," said Gene Rudd, associate executive director of the Christian Medical Association.

Families Opposing Doctors

Beginning last March [2005], Donna Jandras, of Bethlehem, Penn., wrangled for 10 weeks with doctors at Lehigh Valley Hospital to do everything possible to keep alive her mother Loretta, 92, after a heart attack. But, backed by the institution's ethics committee, Lehigh's medical staff declined and placed a Do Not Resuscitate (DNR) order on Loretta's chart. Mrs. Jandras fought to have it removed. In the end, Mrs. Jandras had her mother transferred to another facility, where she died the next day.

In April 2005, the family of Spiro Nikolouzos, 68, succeeded in having him transferred back to a nursing home after a Houston hospital first removed his feeding tube, then threatened to remove his ventilator on the grounds that his condition was hopeless.

The medical profession has long held that doctors are not obligated to offer or even discuss treatment they consider scientifically futile. Over the past 40 years, light-year leaps in health-care technology have enabled physicians to save thousands of patients who couldn't be saved before.

Sometimes, those patients are breathing, but not conscious. Or barely conscious and in scorching pain. Or, like Mrs. Schiavo, conscious but profoundly brain-damaged. In a subset of such cases, patients, their families, or surrogates demand treatment doctors sincerely believe will be "futile" at best, and at worst, will harm the patient further.

"There are going to be times when a doctor, even a doctor committed to life-honoring treatment, will be expected to do something that is totally unreasonable from a scientific perspective," said Dr. Rudd. "The healthcare community has to have some latitude to exercise scientific judgment."

New Motivations for Denying Treatment

But now, new motivations—philosophical and economic—have entered the mix: Does keeping this patient alive jibe with medical "justice," a socialistic version of legitimate concerns over the allocation of health care resources? Will the patient have a "quality of life" the doctor deems acceptable? And under one poisonous rubric, known as "personhood theory," is the patient any longer a person at all? Meanwhile, in the context of stratospheric medical costs, the pressure to discharge patients quickly and send out a bill can affect life-or-death decisions.

At least three states—California, Texas, and Virginia—have passed laws that allow physicians to withhold or deny treatment over the objections of patients' families and surrogates. A growing number of medical facilities have installed "palliative care" units staffed with doctors and nurses who comfort instead of treat. In 2002, the number of such units had climbed to 951, or nearly one in five facilities, over 580 in 2000, according to the American Hospital Association. In addition, patient-doctor conflicts are resolved increasingly by ethics committees, some of whom lean heavily on "quality of life" and personhood theory in rendering decisions.

Hospital Policies Control Futile Care Decisions

Meanwhile, individual hospitals are instituting policies controlling futile-care and DNR decisions. At the Medical University of South Carolina (MUSC), for example, if two doctors agree that a patient should not be resuscitated, they may issue a DNR order regardless of whether the family or surrogate objects.

When hospitals institute such policies, no announcement is made, said Wesley J. Smith, an attorney with the International Task Force on Euthanasia and Assisted Suicide. "Indeed, the first time most learn of these matters is if they come up against a desire to terminate wanted life-sustaining treatment."

When disputes arise, they look something like this: A patient's family member wants doctors to render care that the doctors deem "futile" or "inappropriate." Medical staff, chaplains, social workers, and bioethicists will first try informally to resolve the problem. If neither side cedes ground, the matter will go before the hospital's bioethics committee. If the committee nixes the care the patient's family wants, the patient is left to die, unless the family fights for a transfer to another facility, or in court.

Mr. Smith noted, the majority of physicians "are overwhelmingly dedicated to the well-being and proper care of their patients." But, he said, that doesn't mean to blindly trust, as Kay McClanahan found out.

Futility Is the Opposite of Physician-Assisted Suicide

Those who still believe that the rise of the end-of-life movement is solely due to the quest for increased patient autonomy, and that it has nothing to do with cost, need look no further than the issue of "medical futility." From the standpoint of autonomy, medical futility is the flip side of advance directives and physician-assisted suicide. For medical futility is the issue of what to do about the patient who is demanding care that the medical establishment has deemed "futile" (i.e., extremely unlikely to be beneficial).

If autonomy were really the only issue, then the people who stand foursquare behind the autonomy of the patient when urging her to establish an advance directive or when she seeks physician-assisted suicide would also strongly support her when she wants to express her autonomy by asking for *more* care. But that's not what is happening. . . .

When autonomy and cost both support the same side of an issue, it's easy for everybody to say they're supporting autonomy. It's only when autonomy and cost are on opposite sides of an issue that we can see what's really the principle motivator.

Richard N. Fogoros, "Grand Unification Theory
of Health Care: Rationing and Death,"
Your Doctor in the Family.com, 2000.
www.yourdoctorinthefamily.com.

McClanahan Case Illustrates Futile Care Policies

In April 2004, Bill McClanahan, 74, a retired federal intelligence officer, took his wife out to dinner then suffered a cardiac arrest. Medics were able to revive him. But Mrs. Mc-

Clanahan now charges that doctors at MUSC immediately diagnosed Mr. McClanahan as a vegetable, then consistently ignored signs of improvement, withheld treatment (even for pneumonia), and urged her to let him die.

One doctor, Mrs. McClanahan said, told her she felt "an ethical duty" not to treat Mr. McClanahan because he would experience an "impaired quality of life." The same doctor, Mrs. McClanahan says, put a DNR order on her husband's chart against her wishes. When she objected, she says the attending physician told her about MUSC's two-doctor override policy.

"Bill was looking at me, smiling at me, coming back to me, yet somebody else had decided he would be better off dead. They told me that," Mrs. McClanahan said. "It was amazing how determined they were not to be proven wrong."

Mrs. McClanahan said she felt powerless against the array of MUSC doctors, legal personnel, and ethics committee members who, she said, agreed Mr. McClanahan should be allowed to die.

MUSC Medical Director John Heffner told WORLD that according to South Carolina law, when a patient is incapacitated, the hierarchy of authority for medical decision-making begins with the spouse. He also said he did "not have knowledge of those conversations" that led to the DNR order for Mr. McClanahan.

Asked whether it was true that his staff had encouraged Mrs. McClanahan to let her husband die, Dr. Heffner said, "I don't have firsthand knowledge of that. I'm sure a lot of caring comments were made and taken out of context."

Mrs. McClanahan said Dr. Heffner "answers questions like a politician." Last month [April 2005], a Tennessee internist accepted care of her husband at a hospital where, Mrs. McClanahan reports, doctors and nurses are rendering compassionate care.

The Emergence of Patient Autonomy

The definition of "caring" is at the root of the futile-care controversy. A growing number of physicians and medical ethicists opine that it is more compassionate to live and let die than to let live. It is in part the concept of medical futility, or "futile care," that drives this.

Prior to the 1950s, doctors—carrying admittedly fewer cures in their bags—exercised total control. Regarded by many as small-G gods in white coats, they generally ordered or denied treatment they deemed fit, and patients had little voice in the matter. But in the 1960s and '70s, the concept of "patient autonomy" emerged, and a series of court cases—*Roe v. Wade* [which legalized abortion] among them—established the general principle that Americans have a right to control what is done to their bodies. That sent the ethical pendulum hurtling toward an untenable ethic of absolute patient autonomy.

About 15 years ago, doctors and ethicists began debating the concept of medical futility, partly as a way to reclaim some authority. But the concept proved an unwieldy beast as ideas on what, exactly, constituted "futile" were as varied as the details in each patient's case file. Attempts to neatly package any set of guiding principles or protocols proved—well, futile. In 1994 the American Medical Association issued an opinion that "denial of treatment should be justified by . . . openly stated ethical principles and acceptable standards of care . . . not on the concept of 'futility,' which cannot be meaningfully defined." Acceptable standards, the AMA stated, included resource allocation and quality of life.

Studies Demonstrate Alarming Trends

Today, medical literature treats futile-care theory as unworkable in practice. But the theory lives on in disguise as the literature remains rife with discussions of medical "justice" (which used to mean nondiscrimination on the basis of race or ability to pay, but now means giving preferential care to those more likely to recover), "quality of life," and "person-hood."

In a 2003 study published in the *Journal of Paediatrics and Child Health,* David Isaacs of the Children's Hospital of Westmead in Australia concluded that "a person-centered approach [to brain death] can identify some humans, such as those in a persistent vegetative state, whose continued existence has lost value and whose lives we are not obliged to sustain."

A 2003 study by Swiss doctors found an unacceptable "cost per survivor" among intensive-care patients with hospital stays of longer than seven days. "Resource use per patient surviving the ICU was approximately 10-fold higher in patients with [a] long-term stay.... Further, quality of life has also to be taken into account.... To justify resource use for those with an extremely long stay, more needs to be known about the outcome of these individuals."

A 2005 study published in *Ethics in Cardiopulmonary Medicine* argues that it is not always necessary to allow a mentally competent but sedated terminal patient to participate in end-of-life decision-making. It is not always compassionate, argues author Mark R. Tonelli, to wake them up only to tell them they are dying.

When pernicious material in "the literature" reaches critical mass, the effect can be disastrous, said Christian Medical Association's Dr. Rudd, as has happened with "scientific" discussions of homosexuality, pedophilia, and assisted suicide, issues European researchers systematically destigmatized before sending them West.

American medicine now teeters on the edge of a dangerous utilitarian ethic: "Medicine has moved away from a covenant relationship to more of a contractual relationship that hinges on issues of economics and burdens on the health-care system," Dr. Rudd said. "Any life-honoring value system we still have might succumb to economic pressure. We have to shore up the value system now so that won't happen."

"*[A living will] takes away the decision from medical professionals and family members, and gives individuals the power to choose and decide the precise circumstances of discontinuing treatments.*"

Living Wills Allow Patients to Control When Life Support Stops

Ruthe C. Ashley

Ruthe Ashley, a nurse for fifteen years before becoming a lawyer, argues in the following viewpoint that durable powers of attorney for health care and living wills are essential for making a patient's wishes known regarding medical decisions and end-of-life care. The durable power of attorney allows people to appoint someone they trust to make health care decisions for them should they become incapacitated, which is far preferable than to have strangers make these decisions in the absence of such a document. Living wills, she believes, ensure that a patient's desires about treatment and life support will take precedence over the wishes of doctors or family members.

As you read, consider the following questions:

Ruthe C. Ashley, "Why Are Advance Directives Legally Important?" *Critical Care Nurse*, vol. 25, August 2005. Copyright © 2005 by *Critical Care Nurse*. Reproduced by permission.

Gamble. © 2005 by Ed Gamble. Reproduced by permission.

1. What is conservatorship also called, according to Ashley?
2. Which does the author say is more likely, permanent disability or death?
3. When does Ashley say a living will takes effect?

Advance directives are composed of 2 legal documents: the Durable Power of Attorney for Health Care and a Living Will. A Durable Power of Attorney for Health Care is a legal document appointing a person (or persons) of your choosing to make healthcare decisions for you if you become unable to do so because of injury, illness, or diminished capacity. This document is specific to healthcare decisions and is not the same as a general Durable Power of Attorney, which focuses on nonhealthcare decisions. The Durable Power of Attorney for Health Care is used to provide continued management of your affairs.

The Problems with Having No Decision-maker

Without a Durable Power of Attorney for Health Care and if no one steps forward to make decisions on your behalf, a court may appoint a conservator. Conservatorship is often referred to as a "Living Probate" because it is handled by the probate court and is subject to many of the same problems as probate, including the following:

Loss of Control: The court, not the family or friends, will make decisions for the incapacitated individual. The court can choose a spouse or other family member, or someone known to the incapacitated individual for the conservatorship. However, the court could also choose someone completely unknown to the individual or family. This has happened in cases, such as the [Terri] Schiavo case, in which family members were disputing what should be done with the incapacitated individual. This relationship with the court continues for the rest of the individual's life or until the unlikely event that this person is declared competent.

Cost: Attorney fees and costs will be paid for with the funds available through the individual or family. As long as the relationship continues, fees and costs will continue to accrue. This cost can easily reach thousands of dollars.

Loss of Privacy: All court proceedings regarding a conservatorship are a matter of public record.

Believing that a conservatorship will be unnecessary can be dangerous. In any given year, an individual is far more likely to become permanently disabled than to die. For anyone who wishes to be treated with dignity under such circumstances, conservatorship is not a desirable alternative.

The Five Wishes: Living Will

The *Five Wishes* Form was created by Aging with Dignity, Inc., as a Florida advance directive in 1997....

Wish 1. The person I want to make care decisions for me when I can't. This section gives guidance on whom to pick as an agent and includes a list of powers of the agent.

Wish 2: My wish for the kind of medical treatment I want or don't want. This section describes what "life-support treatment" means, and addresses whether one wants it or does not want....

Wish 3: My wish for how comfortable I want to be. This section addresses comfort steps such as massage, music, and warm baths, along with pain and symptom management.

Wish 4: My wish for how I want people to treat me. This section addresses desires to have others present, being touched and talked to, being cared for with kindness and cheerfulness, among other matters.

Wish 5: My wish for what I want my loved ones to know. This section includes a number of messages of love, forgiveness, acceptance of death, holding of good memories, and prompts for funeral wishes or memorials, disposition of remains, and organ donation if desired.

Charles P. Sabatino, National Academy of Elder Law Attorneys Journal, 2005.

The Benefits of Living Wills

The second document that makes up Advance Directives is a Living Will. With this legal document, a person can declare which medical procedures he or she wants or does not want

performed when terminally ill or in a persistent vegetative state. Generally, the Living Will applies only to comatose patients who can no longer communicate their wishes to terminate life support systems. This document is called "living" because, unlike testamentary wills, it takes effect before death. A Living Will is often called a "right-to-die" or "death-with-dignity" form.

A Living Will provides important legal protections for healthcare professionals, and communicates the individual's wishes to the family and the designated Durable Power of Attorney for Health Care. It takes away the decision from medical professionals and family members, and gives individuals the power to choose and decide the precise circumstances of discontinuing treatments. The Living Will also clearly states who among your loved ones and healthcare providers should have the power to withdraw life support.

Remember, not to decide in advance leaves the door open for someone else to decide for you. . . . At your next family event, gather everyone over the age of 18 and have a signing party. It could save much grief in the future.

| "There is direct evidence that living wills regularly fail to have their intended effect."

Living Wills Fail to Give Patients Control over Life Support

Angela Fagerlin and Carl E. Schneider

The following viewpoint is an excerpt from a report written by researchers Angela Fagerlin and Carl E. Schneider detailing the problems with living wills. Despite the fact that these documents outline a patient's wishes about medical treatment and end-of-life care, Fagerlin and Schneider claim that doctors rarely follow them. According to the authors, such documents fail to have their intended effect because of three reasons: doctors find the instructions too vague to follow; living wills only become activated when death is imminent, but doctors have difficulty identifying when patients are near death; and families of patients often override the wishes expressed in the document. Because of these failings, Fagerlin and Schneider contend that physicians should stop recommending that patients fill out living wills. Fagerlin is a research scientist at the University of Michigan. Carl Schneider is a professor of law and bioethics, also at the University of Michigan.

Angela Fagerlin and Carl E. Schneider, "Enough: The Failure of the Living Will," *Hastings Center Report*, vol. 34, 2004, pp. 30–42. Copyright © 2004 by the Hastings Center. Reproduced by permission.

As you read, consider the following questions:

1. What therapies were doctors most and least likely to withhold under the guidance of a living will?
2. What analysis do Fagerlin and Schneider use to discourage the promotion of living wills?
3. What is one of the benefits of durable powers of attorney instead of living wills?

Enough. The living will has failed, and it is time to say so.

We should have known it would fail: A notable but neglected psychological literature always provided arresting reasons to expect the policy of living wills to misfire. Given their alluring potential, perhaps they were worth trying. But a crescendoing empirical literature and persistent clinical disappointments reveal that the rewards of the campaign to promote living wills do not justify its costs. Nor can any degree of tinkering ever make the living will an effective instrument of social policy. . . .

Living wills are still widely and confidently urged on patients, and they retain the allegiance of many bioethicists, doctors, nurses, social workers, and patients. For these loyal advocates, we offer systematic proof that such persistence in error is but the triumph of dogma over inquiry and hope over experience. . . .

Living Wills Do Not Alter Patient Care

Studies of how living wills are implemented . . . show that living wills seem not to affect patients' treatments. For instance, one study concluded that living wills "do not influence the level of medical care overall. This finding was manifested in the quantitatively equal use of diagnostic testing, operations, and invasive hemodynamic monitoring among patients with and without advance directives. Hospital and ICU lengths of stay, as well as health care costs, were also similar for patients with and without advance directive statements, [wrote M.D. Goodman and collegues]" Another study found that in thirty of thirty-nine cases in which a patient was incompetent and the living will was in the patient's medical record, the surrogate decisionmaker was not the person the patient had appointed. In yet a third study, a quarter of the patients received care that was inconsistent with their living will. . . .

Why don't living wills affect care? Joan Teno and colleagues saw no evidence "that a physician unilaterally decided to ignore or disregard an AD [advance directive]." Rather, there was "a complex interaction of . . . three themes." First, "the contents of ADs were vague and difficult to apply to current clinical situations." The imprecision of living wills not only stymies interpreters, it exacerbates their natural tendency to read documents in light of their own preferences. Thus "(e)ven with the therapy-specific AD accompanied by designation of a proxy and prior patient-physician discussion, the proportion of physicians were willing to withhold therapies was quite variable: cardiopulmonary resuscitation, 100%; administration of artificial nutrition and hydration, 82%; administration of antibiotics, 80%; simple tests, 70%; and administration of pain medication, 13%," [according to W.R. Mower and L.J. Baraff].

Second, the Teno team found that "patients were not seen as 'absolutely, hopelessly ill,' and thus, it was never considered the time to invoke the AD." Living wills typically operate when patients become terminally ill, but neither doctors nor families lightly conclude patients are dying, especially when that means ending treatment. And understandably. For instance, "on the day before death, the median prognosis for patients with heart failure is still a 50% chance to live 6 more months because patients with heart failure typically die quickly from an unpredictable complication like arrhythmia or infection," [wrote Joanne Lynn]. So by the time doctors and families finally conclude the patient is dying, the patient's condi-

What Are Advance Directives?

An advance directive tells your doctor what kind of care you would like to have if you become unable to make medical decisions. . . .

A living will is one type of advance directive. It only comes into effect when you are terminally ill. . . . In a living will, you can describe the kind of treatment you want in certain situations. A living will doesn't let you select someone to make decisions for you. . . .

A durable power of attorney (DPA) for health care is another kind of advance directive. A DPA states whom you have chosen to make health care decisions for you. It becomes active any time you are unconscious or unable to make medical decisions.

"Advance Directives and Do Not
Resuscitate Orders," familydoctor.org,
March 2005. http://familydoctor.org.

tion is already so dire that treatment looks pointless quite apart from any living will. "In all cases in which life-sustaining treatment was withheld or withdrawn, this decision was made after a trial of life-sustaining treatment and at a time when the patient was seen as 'absolutely, hopelessly ill' or 'actively dying.' Until patients crossed this threshold, ADs were not seen as applicable." Thus "it is not surprising that our previous research has shown that those with ADs did not differ in timing of DNR orders or patterns of resource utilization from those without AD, [in the words of Joan Teno]."

Third, "family members or the surrogate designated in a [durable power of attorney] were not available, were ineffectual, or were overwhelmed with their own concerns and did not effectively advocate for the patient." Family members are crucial surrogates because they should be: patients commonly want them to be; they commonly want to be; they specially cherish the patient's interests. Doctors ordinarily assume families know the patient's situation and preferences and may not relish responsibility for life-and-death decisions, and doctors intent on avoiding litigation may realize that the only plausible plaintiffs are families. The family, however, may not direct attention to the advance directive and may not insist on its enforcement. In fact, surrogates may be guided by either their own treatment preferences or an urgent desire to keep their beloved alive.

In ... there is direct evidence that living wills regularly fail to have their intended effect. . . . And if living wills do not affect treatment, they do not work. . . .

Power of Attorney Instead of Living Wills

The cost-benefit analysis here is simple: If living wills lack detectable benefits, they cannot justify any cost, much less the considerable costs they now exact. Any attempt to increase their incidence and their availability to surrogates must be expensive. . . .

If living wills have failed, we must say so. We must say so to patients. If we believe our declamations about truth-telling, we should frankly warn patients how faint is the chance that living wills can have their intended effect. More broadly, we should abjure programs intended to cajole everyone into signing living wills. . . .

Of course we recognize the problems presented by the decisions that must be made for incompetent patients, and our counsel is not wholly negative. Patients anxious to control future medical decisions should be told about durable powers of attorney. These surely do not guarantee patients that their wishes will blossom into fact, but nothing does. What matters is that powers of attorney have advantages over living wills. First, the choices that powers of attorney demand of patients are relatively few, familiar, and simple. Second, a regime of powers of attorney requires little change from current practice, in which family members ordinarily act informally for incompetent patients. Third, powers of attorney probably improve decisions for patients, since surrogates know more at the time of the decision than patients can know in advance. Fourth, powers of attorney are cheap; they require only a simple form easily filled out with little advice. Fifth, powers of attorney can be supplemented by legislation (already in force in some states) akin to statutes of intestacy. These statutes specify who is to act for incompetent patients who have not specified a surrogate. In short, durable powers of attorney are—as these things go—simple, direct, modest, straightforward, and thrifty.

In social policy as in medicine, plausible notions can turn out to be bad ideas. Bad ideas should be renounced. Bloodletting once seemed plausible, but when it demonstrably failed, the course of wisdom was to abandon it, not to insist on its virtues and to scrounge for alternative justifications for it. Living wills were praised and peddled before they were fully developed, much less studied. They have now failed repeated tests of practice. It is time to say, "enough."

Periodical Bibliography

The following articles have been selected to supplement the diverse views presented in this chapter.

J. David Bleich — "The Physician as a Conscientious Objector," *Fordham Urban Law Journal*, November 2002.

Eric Cohen — "What Living Wills Won't Do: The Limits of Autonomy," *Weekly Standard*, April 18, 2005.

Commonweal — "Allowing to Die," November 7, 2003. www-.commonwealmagazine.org.

Michael Gougis — "Living Will Lets Cancer Patients Avoid Agony," *Los Angeles Daily News*, November 2, 2003.

Ronald Hamel and Michael Panicola — "Must We Preserve Life? The Narrowing of Traditional Catholic Teaching," *America*, April 19, 2004.

Ben Hyink — "Personhood Rights," Institute for Ethics and Emerging Technologies, May 25, 2005. www.ieet.org.

John Leo — "An Autopsy Won't End It," *U.S. News & World Report*, June 27, 2005.

Thomas A. Shannon and James J. Walter — "Assisted Nutrition and Hydration and the Catholic Tradition," *Theological Studies*, September 2005.

Wesley J. Smith — "Doc Knows Best," *National Review Online*, January 6, 2003. www.nationalreview.com.

James L. Werth Jr. — "Concerns About Decisions Related to Withholding/Withdrawing Life-Sustaining Treatment and Futility for Persons with Disabilities," *Journal of Disability Policy Studies*, June 22, 2005.

YourDoctorintheFamily.com — "Grand Unification Theory of Health Care: Rationing and Death—Covert Rationing and End-of-Life Care," 2000. www.yourdoctorinthe-family.com.

For Further Discussion

Chapter 1

1. Thomas Preston, Martin Gunderson, and David J. Mayo emphasize the importance of autonomy in their argument in favor of euthanasia. They contend that though a patient's decision to request euthanasia may not be perfectly autonomous, no decision fits that criterion. In your view, is this a convincing argument? Do you think a decision to request euthanasia is still valid even if others may be pressuring a patient to elect to die? Is it possible to protect patients from such influence when they are making these kinds of decisions?

2. In his viewpoint, John Shelby Keown maintains that many requests for euthanasia are not truly autonomous. Would even a truly autonomous decision to request euthanasia be acceptable in Keown's view? Explain your answer.

3. Do you think that all physical pain can be relieved with medication? Evaluate this argument in light of the South Australia Voluntary Euthanasia Society's examples of unrelieved suffering. How does your answer affect your view of euthanasia?

4. How do John Shelby Spong and Chris Armstrong differ in their view of the relationship between God and humanity? How do their different conceptions of this relationship affect the conclusions they draw about euthanasia? Which viewpoint do you find to be stronger? Explain.

Chapter 2

1. Roger S. Magnusson argues that if euthanasia were legal, society could better protect patients. Margaret Somer-

ville contends that legalizing euthanasia would harm society. Whose argument do you find more convincing, and why?

2. Both Ira Byock and Timothy E. Quill are practicing physicians, yet they have very different views on what constitutes good end-of-life care. In what ways do the doctors agree? In what ways do they disagree?

3. Yvonne Mak, Glyn Elwyn, and Ilora G. Finlay contend that more studies are needed before assisted suicide is legalized. Do you think their argument is valid? Why or why not? How might more research change the debate on assisted suicide?

Chapter 3

1. John Shelby Keown and Jocelyn Downie both address the slippery slope argument used frequently in euthanasia debates. Which author do you think has analyzed the slippery slope argument to better effect? Explain.

2. Oregon Right to Life and the Death with Dignity National Center make competing claims about the legalization of assisted suicide in Oregon. Which organization do you think is more convincing? Support your answer, using examples from the viewpoints.

3. How does the fact that Barry Corbet is disabled affect your evaluation of his argument? Does the fact that he is disabled strengthen or weaken his argument, in your view? Explain.

Chapter 4

1. Both Wesley J. Smith and John Collins Harvey discuss the persistent vegetative state in their viewpoints. How do their opinions differ on this topic? Do you find either to be overly optimistic or pessimistic about patients in this condition? Explain.

2. Kevin T. Keith argues that hospitals have the right to withdraw treatment in situations they deem futile if a patient cannot pay for it. Would this, in your opinion, be ethical? Why or why not?

3. Ruthe C. Ashley takes a positive view of living wills while Angela Fagerlin and Carl E. Schneider take a much more pessimistic view of their worth. Which argument do you find more convincing, and why?

Organizations to Contact

American Life League
PO Box 1350, Stafford, VA 22555
(540) 659-4171 • fax: (540) 659-2586
Web site: www.all.org

The league believes that human life is sacred. It works to educate the public about the dangers of all forms of euthanasia and opposes legislative efforts that would legalize or increase its incidence. It publishes the bimonthly pro-life magazine *Celebrate Life* and distributes videos, brochures, and newsletters monitoring euthanasia-related developments.

American Society of Law, Medicine, and Ethics
765 Commonwealth Ave., Suite 1634
 Boston, MA 02215
(617) 262-4990 • fax: (617) 437-7596
e-mail: info@aslme.org
Web site: www.aslme.org

The society's members include physicians, attorneys, health care administrators, and others interested in the relationship between law, medicine, and ethics. The organization has an information clearinghouse and a library, and it acts as a forum for discussion on issues such as pain management, euthanasia, and assisted suicide. It publishes the quarterlies *American Journal of Law and Medicine* and *Journal of Law, Medicine, and Ethics*.

Americans for Better Care of the Dying (ABCD)
1700 Diagonal Rd., Suite 635
 Alexandria, VA 22314
(703) 647-8505 • fax: (703) 837-1233
e-mail: info@abcd-caring.org
Web site: www.abcd-caring.org

ABCD, founded in 1997, focuses on improving end-of-life care for all Americans. The group supports improved pain management, better financial reimbursement for medical expenses, enhanced continuity of care between health professionals, and improved help for family caregivers. Its Web site enables users to search the book *Handbook for Mortals: Guidance for People Facing Serious Illness,* and it provides an extensive list of links to other sites about end-of-life care.

Citizens United Resisting Euthanasia (CURE)
303 Truman St., Berkeley Springs
  WV 25411
(304) 258-5433 • fax: (304) 258-5420
e-mail: cureltd@verizon.net
Web site: http://mysite.verizon.net/cureltd/index.html

Founded in 1981, CURE is a nationwide network of concerned citizens of diverse professional, political, and religious backgrounds who oppose euthanasia. CURE publishes *Life Matters* brochures and articles on euthanasia-related topics.

Compassion & Choices
PO Box 101810, Denver, CO 80250-1810
(800) 247-7421 • fax: (303) 639-1224
e-mail: info@compassionandchoices.org
Web site: www.compassionandchoices.org

Compassion & Choices was formed by the 2005 union of two major choice-in-dying groups: Compassion in Dying and End-of-Life Choices. The mission of this group is to work for a change in the laws of the United States to include assisted suicide as a choice at the end of life. They also focus on educating the public and serving clients who desire help with end-of-life decision making. It publishes the quarterly *Compassion & Choices Magazine.*

Death with Dignity National Center (DDNC)
520 SW Sixth Ave., Suite 1030
  Portland, OR 97204
(503) 228-4415 • fax: (503) 228-7454
Web site: www.deathwithdignity.org

Death with Dignity is a nonprofit charitable organization dedicated to increasing the choices and autonomy of terminally ill patients to include assisted suicide. The group successfully spearheaded the law to make assisted suicide legal in Oregon. The organization's goals are to defend this law in Oregon through litigation and lobbying, to mobilize the public through education in order to legalize assisted suicide in other states, and to reach out to medical professionals to bridge the end-of-life education gap. The group publishes a quarterly newsletter called *Dignity Report* .

Euthanasia Prevention Coalition
Box 25033, London   N6C 6A8
   Ontario
(519) 439-3348 • fax: (519) 439-7053
e-mail: euthanasiaprevention@on.aibn.com
Web site: www.epcc.ca

The Euthanasia Prevention Coalition opposes the promotion or legalization of euthanasia and assisted suicide. The coalition's purpose is to educate the public on risks associated with the promotion of euthanasia, increase public awareness of alternative methods for the relief of pain and suffering, and to represent the vulnerable as an advocate before the courts on euthanasia issues. The group produces pamphlets and bulletin inserts to promote opposition to euthanasia.

Euthanasia Research and Guidance Organization (ERGO)
24829 Norris Ln., Junction City
   OR   97448-9559
(541) 998-1873
e-mail: ergo@efn.org
Web site: www.finalexit.org

ERGO is a nonprofit educational group that advocates for assisted dying for persons who are terminally or hopelessly ill and wish to end their suffering. ERGO develops and publishes guidelines for patients and physicians to better prepare them to make life-ending decisions. The organization is run by Derek Humphry, who also moderates ERGO's free daily news digest of right-to-die information from around the world.

Human Life International (HLI)
4 Family Life Ln., Front Royal, VA   22630
(540) 635-7884 • fax: (540) 622-6247
e-mail: hli@hli.org
Web site: www.hli.org

HLI rejects euthanasia and believes assisted suicide is morally unacceptable, based on the teachings of the Roman Catholic Church. It defends the rights of the unborn, the disabled, and those threatened by euthanasia; and it provides education, advocacy, and support services. HLI publishes the monthly newsletters *HLI Special Report* and *HLI Front Lines*. The group's position statement on euthanasia is available online, and a number of cassette tapes on the issue are available through their Web site.

International Task Force on Euthanasia and Assisted Suicide
PO Box 760, Steubenville, OH   43952
(740) 282-3810
e-mail: info@iaetf.org
Web site: www.iaetf.org

The International Task Force is a nonprofit organization that opposes euthanasia, assisted suicide, and policies that threaten the lives of the medically vulnerable. The group publishes fact sheets and position papers on euthanasia-related topics in addition to the bimonthly newsletter *Update*. They also analyze policies and legislation regarding end-of-life issues and file amicus curiae briefs in court cases when appropriate. Much detailed information about euthanasia is available for immediate access through the group's Web site.

National Hospice and Palliative Care Organization (NHPCO)
1700 Diagonal Rd., Suite 625, Alexandria, VA   22314

(703) 837-1500 • fax: (703) 837-1233
e-mail: nhpco_info@nhpco.org
Web site: www.nhpco.org

The NHPCO works to educate the public about the benefits of hospice and palliative care for the terminally ill and their families. Its members believe that with the proper care and pain medication, the terminally ill can live out their lives comfortably and in the company of their families. The organization opposes euthanasia and assisted suicide, and it maintains a Web site dedicated to providing free information about end-of-life issues called Caring Connections (www.caringinfo .org).

National Right to Life Committee (NRLC)
512 Tenth St. NW, Washington, DC   20004
(202) 626-8800
e-mail: NRLC@nrlc.org
Web site: www.nrlc.org

The NRLC is opposed to assisted suicide and euthanasia. The organization works to educate its members and the public about the potential dangers of legalized assisted suicide and euthanasia, and has led a drive called "Will to Live" for those who wish to emphasize that they would want food and water provided to them if they become unable to speak for themselves. Their Web site provides information on why they oppose euthanasia and assisted suicide, what can be done for those in severe pain, and arguments against causing death through dehydration and starvation. It publishes a monthly newsletter, *NRL News*, which is also available online, with archives going back to 1998.

Not Dead Yet (NDY)
7521 Madison St., Forest Park, IL   60130
(708) 209-1500 • fax: (708) 209-1735
e-mail: ndycoleman@aol.com
Web site: www.notdeadyet.org

Not Dead Yet is a disability-rights group founded in 1996 that focuses on opposing legal assisted suicide and euthanasia. The group believes that making these practices legal would violate the Americans with Disabilities Act because it singles out certain individuals based on their health status. NDY lobbies elected officials, joins with like-minded organizations in relevant court cases, and publicly protests. Fact sheets, press releases, and information about court cases are available on NDY's Web site.

Ontario Consultants on Religious Tolerance (OCRT)

Box 27026, Kingston, Ontario
  ONT K7M 8W5
  Canada
fax: (613) 547-9015
e-mail: ocrt@religioustolerance.org
Web site: www.religioustolerance.org

The OCRT does not take a position for or against euthanasia or other controversial issues but presents information from multiple perspectives. Its primary activity is maintaining a Web site that covers many topics, including euthanasia and assisted suicide. The online resource covers ethical and religious aspects of euthanasia.

Oregon Right to Life (ORTL)

4335 River Rd. North, Salem, OR   97303
(503) 463-8563 • fax: (503) 463-8564
e-mail: ortl@ortl.org
Web site: www.ortl.org

Oregon Right to Life opposes euthanasia and assisted suicide. Because Oregon is the only state that has legalized assisted suicide, ORTL's Web site includes detailed information opposing the practice in that state, including a link to the annual reports on Oregon's Death with Dignity Act and critiques of the details of the law. It publishes *Life in Oregon* bimonthly, with archives online dating back to 2001.

South Australian Voluntary Euthanasia Society (SAVES)
PO Box 2151, Kent Town   SA 5071,
   Australia
fax: 61 8 8265 2287
e-mail: info@saves.asn.au
Web site: www.saves.asn.au

SAVES is an organization that supports the legalization of voluntary euthanasia with appropriate safeguards. The group works to raise community awareness about the need for euthanasia, correct misinformation about the practice, engage and educate medical professionals, inform members of their end-of-life health care rights under the current law, and lobby government officials for the legalization of euthanasia. It publishes *VE Bulletin* three times a year and maintains a Web site with numerous fact sheets and bulletin archives dating back to 1997.

Voluntary Euthanasia Society (VES)
13 Prince of Wales Terrace, London   W8 5PG
   United Kingdom
020 7937 7770 • fax: 020 7376 2648
e-mail: info@ves.org.uk
Web site: www.ves.org.uk

The VES is a UK-based organization that campaigns for greater choice at the end of life, including the right to receive help to die for those with a terminal illness. The group lobbies Parliament to pass laws for these rights, and defends the rights of patients who do not want life-prolonging medical treatment. Their Web site includes information about living wills as well as press releases and other resources related to euthanasia.

Bibliography of Books

Margaret P. Battin, David Mayo, and Susan Wolf, eds.
Physician-Assisted Suicide: Pro and Con. Lanham, MD: Rowman & Littlefield, 2002.

Nigel Biggar
Aiming to Kill: The Ethics of Suicide and Euthanasia . Cleveland, OH: Pilgrim Press, 2004.

Hazel Biggs
Euthanasia: Death with Dignity and the Law. Oxford, England: Hart, 2002.

Jonathan E. Brockopp, ed.
Islamic Ethics of Life: Abortion, War, and Euthanasia. Columbia: University of South Carolina Press, 2003.

Ira Byock
The Four Things That Matter Most: A Book About Living . New York: Simon & Schuster, 2004.

Paul Chamberlain
Final Wishes: A Cautionary Tale on Death, Dignity, and Physician-Assisted Suicide. Downers Grove, IL: InterVarsity Press, 2000.

Raphael Cohen-Almagor
Euthanasia in the Netherlands: The Policy and Practice of Mercy Killing. New York: Springer, 2004.

Miriam Cosic
The Right to Die: An Examination of the Euthanasia Debate. London: New Holland, 2003.

Diego De Leo, ed.
Suicide and Euthanasia in Older Adults: A Transcultural Journey. Cambridge, MA: Hogrefe & Huber, 2001.

Ian Robert
Dowbiggin

A Concise History of Euthanasia: Life, Death, God, and Medicine. Lanham, MD: Rowman & Littlefield, 2005.

Ian Robert
Dowbiggin

A Merciful End: The Euthanasia Movement in Modern America . New York: Oxford University Press, 2002.

Jocelyn Downie

Dying Justice: A Case for Decriminalizing Euthanasia in Canada. Toronto: University of Toronto Press, 2004.

William Dudley, ed.

Euthanasia: Examining Issues Through Political Cartoons . San Diego: Greenhaven Press, 2002.

Arthur J. Dyck

Life's Worth: The Case Against Assisted Suicide . Grand Rapids, MI: Eerdmans, 2002.

Louis Flancbaum

"And You Shall Live by Them": Contemporary Jewish Approaches to Medical Ethics. Pittsburgh: Mirkov, 2001.

Kathleen M. Foley
and Herbert
Hendin

The Case Against Assisted Suicide: For the Right to End-of-Life Care. Baltimore: Johns Hopkins University Press, 2002.

Derek Humphry

Final Exit: The Practicalities of Self-Deliverance and Assisted Suicide for the Dying. Third Ed. Surrey, England: Delta, 2002.

Derek Humphry

The Good Euthanasia Guide 2005: Where, What, and Who in Choices in Dying. Junction City, OR: Norris Lane Press/ERGO, 2005.

Sharon R. Kaufman — *And a Time to Die: How American Hospitals Shape the End of Life.* New York: Simon & Schuster, 2005.

John Keown — *Euthanasia, Ethics, and Public Policy: An Argument Against Legalisation.* Cambridge, England: Cambridge University Press, 2002.

Madeline Kisha and Paula Andrasko — *Free Rein to Kill: Euthanasia in America.* Lincoln, NE: iUniverse, 2005.

L.M. Kopelman and K.A. de Ville, eds. — *Physician-Assisted Suicide: What Are the Issues?* New York: Springer, 2001.

Shai J. Lavi — *The Modern Art of Dying: A History of Euthanasia in the United States.* Princeton, NJ: Princeton University Press, 2005.

John R. Ling — *The Edge of Life: Dying, Death, and Euthanasia.* Leominster, England: DayOne, 2003.

Roger S. Magnusson — *Angels of Death: Exploring the Euthanasia Underground* . New Haven, CT: Yale University Press, 2002.

William F. May — *Testing the Medical Covenant: Active Euthanasia and Health Care Reform.* Eugene, OR: Wipf & Stock, 2004.

Tom Meulenberg and Paul Schotsman, eds. — *Euthanasia and Palliative Care in the Low Countries* . Leuven, Belgium: Peeters, 2005.

Philip Nitschke
and Fiona Stewart

Killing Me Softly: Voluntary Euthanasia and the Road to the Peaceful Pill.
Victoria, Australia: Penguin, 2005.

Oregon
Department of
Health and
uman Services,
Office of Disease
Prevention and
Epidemiology

Seventh Annual Report on Oregon's Death with Dignity Act. March 2005.

Timothy E. Quill
and Margaret P.
Battin, eds.

Physician-Assisted Dying: The Case for Palliative Care and Patient Choice.
Baltimore: Johns Hopkins University Press, 2004.

Barry Rosenfeld

Assisted Suicide and the Right to Die: The Interface of Social Science, Public Policy, and Medical Ethics. Washington, DC: American Psychological Association, 2004.

Carl E. Schneider

Law at the End of Life: The Supreme Court and Assisted Suicide. Ann Arbor: University of Michigan Press, 2000.

Wesley J. Smith

Culture of Death: The Assault on Medical Ethics in America. San Francisco: Encounter Books, 2000.

Wesley J. Smith

Forced Exit: Euthanasia, Assisted Suicide, and the New Duty to Die. San Francisco: Encounter Books, 2005.

Lois Snyder and
Arthur L. Caplan,
eds.

Assisted Suicide: Finding Common Ground. Bloomington: Indiana University Press, 2001.

Margaret Somerville	*Death Talk: The Case Against Euthanasia and Physician-Assisted Suicide.* Montreal: McGill-Queen's University Press, 2001.
Margaret Somerville	*The Ethical Canary: Science, Society, and the Human Spirit.* Toronto: Penguin Books Canada, 2000.
William F. Sullivan	*Eye of the Heart: Knowing the Human Good in the Euthanasia Debate.* Toronto: University of Toronto Press, 2005.
Arthur Gordon Svenson and Susan M. Behuniak	*Physician-Assisted Suicide: The Anatomy of a Constitutional Law Issue.* Lanham, MD: Rowman & Littlefield, 2002.
Torbjörn Tännsjö, ed.	*Terminal Sedation: Euthanasia in Disguise?* New York: Springer, 2004.
Henk Ten Have and Jos Welie	*Death and Medical Power: An Ethical Analysis of Dutch Euthanasia Practice.* Berkshire, England: Open University Press, 2005.
Gail Tulloch	*Euthanasia: Choice and Death.* Scotland: Edinburgh University Press, 2005.

Index

abortion, 132, 134–35

Adamson, Kate, 215–17

advance directives, 31, 62, 174–75, 225, 240

    types of, 239, 246

    see also power of attorney

"Allowing Death and Taking Life: Withholding or Withdrawing Artificially Administered Nutrition and Hydration" (Evangelical Lutheran Church), 21

American Civil Liberties Union (ACLU), 214

American Medical Association (AMA), 236

Americans with Disabilities Act (1990), 195

Annals of Internal Medicine (journal), 50

Armstrong, Chris, 20

artificial life support

    tube feeding as, 202–204

    see also treatment

Ashcroft, John, 51, 178

Ashley, Ruthe C., 238

Balch, Burke J., 44

Baraff, L.J., 245

Barnett, Erin Hoover, 160

Batavia, Andrew I., 188

Batavia, Drew, 177, 178

Battin, Margaret P., 103

Berry, Zail, 48

Bible, 24, 28

Book of Discipline (United Methodist Church), 21

Borthwick, C.J., 217

British Medical Journal, 14

Brock, Dan, 15–16

Brownlow, Suzanne, 51

Burger, Rick, 47–48

Burke, William, 214–15

Bush, Jeb, 213

Byock, Ira, 96, 97

Callahan, D., 80, 90

Canterbury v. Spence (1972), 187

Caplan, Arthur, 48, 90

Case Against Assisted Suicide, The (Kamisar), 76

Cassel, Christine K., 50

Cheney, Kate, 159–60

Chochinov, Harvey Max, 49

Christianity, 21

    should change views on death, 28–30

Chun, Trudy, 40

Concerned Women for America, 40

Controlled Substances Act, 170–71

Corbet, Barry, 172

Cranford, Ronald, 215

Crew, Reginald, 115, 116

Crick, Nancy, 84

Crossley, R., 217

Currow, David, 51–52

Death Talk (Somerville), 79

Death with Dignity National Center (DDNC), 163

dehydration, 34, 166, 207

    as potentially painful death, 214–15

den Hartogh, Govert, 93

disabled, 181, 188

    opposition to euthanasia among, 70, 175–77

        is based on medical vitalism, 191–92

    self-determination is core value for, 194–96

diseases

causing suffering without pain, 37–39

causing uncontrollable pain, 34–36

Dowbiffin, Ian, 117

Downie, Jocelyn, 59, 142

Drug Enforcement Administration (DEA), 165–66

Dworkin, Ronald, 67, 194

Dying Well: Peace and Possibilities at the End of Life (Byock), 97

Elwyn, Glyn, 120

Emanuel, Ezekiel J., 50, 117

end-of-life care. *See* palliative care

Ethical Canary, The (Somerville), 18, 78

Ethics in Cardiopulmonary Medicine (journal), 237

euthanasia

application of, to incompetent patients, 139–40

historical opposition to, 24–25

hurts society's most vulnerable members, 83–84

impact of, on medicine, 82–83

as killing, 118–19

legalized

arguments for/against, 121–22

can be controlled, 31–32

con, 135–37

libertarian view of, 115–18

negative consequences of, 23, 79–80, 157–58

in the Netherlands, 46–47, 90–92

is not available on demand, 149–50

is not widespread, 148–49

nonvoluntary administration of, 128, 157

in Nazi Germany, 46, 145–47

nonvoluntary, prevalence of, 152–54

passive allowing of death vs., 21–23

requests for, may not be autonomous, 72–73

research on, 121, 122–23

see also physician-assisted suicide

Euthanasia, Ethics and Public Policy: An Argument for Legalization (Keown), 130

Evangelical Lutheran Church, 21

Fagerlin, Angela, 243

families

demand for aggressive treatment by, 226–27, 231–32

enforcement of advance directive and, 246–47

Fenigsen, Richard, 148–49, 151

Finlay, Ilora G., 120

Fletcher, Joseph, 45

Fogoros, Richard N., 234

Fournier, Keith, 45

Fourteenth Amendment, 45

Freeland, Michael, 160–61

Gallagher, Hugh, 178, 179

Gaylin, W., 82

Gill, Robin, 30

Girsh, Faye, 174

Goodman, M.D., 245

Gordon, Steve, 96

Griffiths, John, 153

Gunderson, Martin, 53, 184, 185

Gunning, Karel, 47

Harvey, John Collins, 201

Hedley, Mark, 230
Heffner, John, 235
Hendlin, Herbert, 147
Hentoff, Nat, 47
Hippocratic Oath, 49
Hippocratic School, 24
Hitler, Adolf, 46
human life, 131
    opposing views on, 80–81
    value of, medical vitalism and,
        186–89
Humphry, Derek, 91

In Defense of Life (Fournier and
    Watkins), 45
informed consent, 60, 62, 63
    is safeguard against involun-
        tary euthanasia, 144
    con, 174
    medical vitalism vs., 186–88
    strengthening safeguards for,
        192–93
Isaacs, David, 237
Islam, 22

Jandras, Donna, 231
Jennett, Bryan, 217
Jochemson, Henk, 83
Johnson, Harriet McBryde, 176,
    179
*Journal of Paediatrics and Child
    Health,* 237

Kamisar, Yale, 76, 137
*Kate's Journal: Triumph over Ad-
    versity* (Adamson), 216
Katz, J., 84
Keith, Kevin T., 224
Kelly, Gerald, 210
Keown, John Shelby, 65, 130, 151
Kevorkian, Jack, 42–43, 178
King, Patricia A., 123

Kissane, David, 72

Lancet (journal), 49
Lee, Daniel E., 100
Lee v. Oregon (1997), 156, 158
Lewis, C.S., 42
Linacre Center for Healthcare Eth-
    ics, 157
living wills, 241, 242
    problems with, 244–47
Lynn, Joanne, 245

Magnusson, Roger S., 85
Mak, Yvonne, 120
Mann, Patricia S., 134
Martin, Michael, 220
Matheny, Patrick, 159
Mayo, David J., 53, 184
McClanahan, Bill, 234–35
medical futility, 236
    hospitals control decisions on,
        232–33
    resource scarcity and, 227–28
Medical Journal of Australia, 48
medical vitalism, 191–92
Mower, W.R., 245

New York Times (newspaper), 45
Nickles, Don, 51
Nighbert, Marjorie, 221–22
Nikolouzos, Spiro, 231

Oregon Death with Dignity law,
    105, 164
    early cases under, 158–61
    has been a failure, 161–62
    has not undermined health
        care, 166–67
    inconsistencies in, 180–81
    opposition to, 51–52
    safeguards in, 128–29, 167

are adequate, 168–69
utilization of, 16, 84, 106
Oregon Right to Life (ORTL), 155
O'Reilly Factor, The (TV series), 216

pain/suffering, 15, 44, 104
diseases causing, 34–39
unbearable
difficulty in defining, 122–23
is not a logical criterion for euthanasia, 140–41
undertreatment of, 49, 165–66
palliative care, 18, 34, 50, 92–93, 101, 124, 188
Parris, Matthew, 114
Patient as a Person, The (Ramsey), 218
patient autonomy, 15–16, 54, 187, 236
extreme individualism vs., 60–61
is core value for disabled, 194–96
limits to, 67–71
need for control vs., 61–62
self-centeredness vs., 62–63
patients, terminally ill
decision-making capacity of, 57–60
demand for aggressive treatment of, 226–27
Patient Self-Determination Act (1990), 188
Paul, Saint, 28
Payne, Richard, 49
persistent vegetative state, 217
causes of, 204–206
personhood, 45, 219–20
physician-assisted suicide (PAS)

alternatives to, 101–102, 107–108
could improve end-of-life care, 92–93, 111–12
covert, 106–107
prevalence of, 86–88, 165
patient autonomy as argument for, 54–56
public opinion on, 41–42, 76, 117
reasons for choosing, 16, 108–109, 122–23
risk-based arguments against, 185–86
can be addressed through policy, 193–94
safeguards on, 89–90, 91
vulnerability related arguments against, 189–91
Pius XII (pope), 210
Planned Parenthood v. Casey (1992), 43
Plum, Fred, 217
polls. *See* surveys
Portenoy, Russell, 50
power of attorney, 238, 246–48
Preston, Thomas, 53

Quill, Timothy E., 103
Quinlan, Karen Ann, 25, 199, 205

Ramsey, Paul, 218
Reardon, Thomas, 49
Remmelink Report, 150
Reno, Janet, 51
right-to-die, 45
right-to-die movement, 14, 41
Rudd, Gene, 231, 232, 237

Sabatino, Charles P., 241
Schaeffer, Francis, 45
Schiavo, Michael, 213

Schiavo, Terri, 199–200, 213, 230, 231
Schindler, Bob, 213
Schindler, Mary, 213
Schneider, Carl E., 243
Shipman, Harold, 82
Sign for Cain, A (Wertham), 46
Silent World of Doctor and Patient, The (Katz), 84
Singer, Peter, 223
slippery slope arguments, 132, 146
  empirical aspect of, 132–37
    argument against, 144–45
  logical aspect of, 137–39
    argument against, 143–44
Smith, Alexander McCall, 69
Smith, Wesley J., 181, 212
Somerville, Margaret, 18, 78, 79, 93–94
Souter, David, 48
South Australian Voluntary Euthanasia Society (SAVES), 33, 105
Spong, John Shelby, 26
Stone, William F., 222
Street, Annette, 72
suffering. *See* pain/suffering
Supreme Court, 45
surveys, 50
  on physician-assisted suicide, 41–42, 76
  of physicians, on participation in assisted suicide, 86–87

Teno, Joan, 245
Tolton, Jere, 222
Tonelli, Mark R., 237
treatment, 232
  living wills do not alter, 244–47
  refusal of, 71, 107, 225
    is same as requesting euthanasia, 43–44
    con, 79

  legal basis of, 43–44
tube feeding, 207
  as artificial life support, 202–203
  financial/emotional costs of, 209–11
  making decisions about ending, 208–209
  withholding, circumstances for, 213–14

United Methodist Church, 21
USA Today (newspaper), 41

Vacco v. Quill (1997), 189
Van Den Haag, Ernest, 45
Vincent, Lynn, 229

Wallace, Marian, 40
Walter, Tony, 14
Washington v. Glucksberg (1997), 156, 195
Waters, Dan, 44
Watkins, William, 45
Wendland. Robert, 215, 220
Wertham, Fredric, 46
What Ever Happened to the Human Race? (Schaeffer), 45
"When Self-Determination Runs Amok" (Callahan), 80
Wolbring, Gregor, 70
Wolf, Leslie E., 123
World Federation of Right to Die Societies, 227
Wyatt, Charlotte, 230
Wyatt, Darren, 230
Wyatt, Debbie, 230

Yablick, Lauri, 174, 175, 180

Zeno, 24